Stud Muffins

Luscious, Delectable, Yummy

(and Good Muffin Recipes, too!)

judi guizado, gilda jimenez, shari hartz, and tammy aldag

gpp

Guilford, Connecticut

Designed by LeAnna Weller Smith

Library of Congress Cataloging-in-Publication Data is available on file.

ISBN: 978-1-59921-354-5

Printed in China

10 9 8 7 6 5 4 3 2 1

To my husband and personal stud muffin, Roy, for all of his support,
endless patience, and IT assistance, and to my children Adam and Rachel,
for their unbelievable willingness to sample many muffin recipes. **— JG**

For the shouldn't, couldn't, wouldn't, and did, thank you.
Most importantly, this is for the bear who believed. **— GJ**

I would like to dedicate this book to my *very* understanding husband,
Dan, my sister Vickie, and brother, Frank, for all of their continued love
and support. Oh, and I can't leave out my two little pups, Gypsy and Maggie,
who watched me patiently at the computer writing stories. **— SH**

To my husband, Steve, to my mom for keeping her doors open
after our late-night shoots, and to my family for their support.
I love you. And to Mike Wise, for all his help. **— TA**

contents

WARNING: may be too hot to handle!

acknowledgments

The authors would like to thank the following for believing in our crazy little idea: Andrea Somberg, our agent-extraordinaire; Ronnie Gramazio and his staff, for their kind support and endless patience; Tammy Aldag, our photographer/ angel and friend; Ted Jimenez; Paul Lambert and Jack Martinez at Ayala Golf Center; John Michael Skulavik; Lisa Guizado; Sheri Shepherd, and all the ladies at Jazzercize; Glenn Miller and his staff at Victoria Gardens; Lauren Lewan; Beckie Moore and Beau; Joseph Filippi Winery; Steve Aldag; Bob Graves at Toll Brothers Homes; Johna Heronime; Richard Klumpp at Body Shots Ultimate Training Center; Mike Wise; all family, friends, and last-minute babysitters; and especially our studs, past and present: John Bazzo, Jack (Sparky) Bell, William Bell, Anthony Bernasconi, Joseph Boehm, Mhanu Boulengier, Catoris Cameron, Emmit Campbell, Branden Gabel, Jeremy Gerdes, Lee Gilbertson, Christopher Hess, Dan Holsten, Jonathan Ibañez, Mark Iszler, Ryan McClanahan, Mark MacDonald, Matt Mendrum, Ron Parnell, Benjamin Roberts, John Romagnoli, Derek Simpson, Stephen Tracey, D.D.S, and Vance Vanevenhoven.

introduction

This book began as a crazy little idea in the minds of some truly desperate housewives. After long, exhausting hours of thinking about men, writing about men, finding men, and oiling down men, the final product you now hold was finally fleshed out.

It was a tough job, but someone had to do it.

a few pre-baking notes from the authors

All of the cooking temperatures throughout *Stud Muffins* are listed using degrees in Fahrenheit. For your convenience, a Fahrenheit-to-Celsius conversion chart is listed below. Happy drool—eh, we mean, baking!

Gas Mark	Fahrenheit	Celsius	Description
1/4	225	110	Very cool/very slow
1/2	250	130	---
1	275	140	cool
2	300	150	---
3	325	170	very moderate
4	350	180	moderate
5	375	190	---
6	400	200	moderately hot
7	425	220	hot
8	450	230	---
9	475	240	very hot

quick tips for baking the *stud muffins* way:

get ready to feel the heat.
Preheat oven to the degree stated on the recipe. Allow ample time for the heat to build from a tiny spark, then swell and rise, ultimately reaching its white-hot peak.

moist is good.
When combining the wet ingredients with the dry ingredients, gently stir until everything is just moistened. This is where a slow, firm hand will give you the results you desire.

seize the moment.
Muffins should be baked soon after mixing. If you wait too long, the ingredients that allow the batter to rise will lose their effectiveness. And nobody is happy when the rise is lost.

size does matter.
Unless otherwise stated, all of the muffin recipes require standard muffin baking cups (approximately 3 inches in diameter and 1¼ inches deep). These muffins will bake to a size that will feel good in your hands. Really good.

can't get your fill?
If the last of the batter doesn't fill all the baking cups, fill empty cups halfway with water before placing pan in the oven, which will allow the last of the muffins to bake properly. Sometimes, quality is much more satisfying than quantity.

make sure you've reached the climax (of baking).
Test muffins for doneness by inserting a toothpick in the center. If it comes out dry, your muffin is ready to be removed from the oven. If there is still batter clinging to the toothpick, continue the baking process, and remember, anticipation can be half the fun.

what a zucchini muffins

makes 12–14 muffins

1½ cups flour

1 cup sugar

½ teaspoon salt

½ teaspoon baking soda

¼ teaspoon baking powder

1 tablespoon cinnamon

½ cup chopped walnuts

2 eggs, slightly beaten

½ cup salted butter, melted

½ teaspoon vanilla

⅓ cup honey

1 cup grated zucchini

1. Preheat oven to 325 degrees.

2. In a large bowl, mix together dry ingredients (flour through walnuts). Form a well in the center. Set aside.

3. In a separate bowl, stir together eggs, butter, vanilla, honey, and zucchini. Pour into dry-ingredient well and stir until just moistened.

4. Lightly grease or paper-line muffin cups. Fill each cup ¾ full. Bake 20 to 25 minutes, or until a toothpick comes out clean.

12

Ripe for the Picking

Sara sat at the side of the road in her car, feebly fanning herself in an attempt to cool down as she waited for the tow truck to come rescue her. It was barely noon, and the temperature was climbing fast. It looked like the heat wave the news had forecasted had arrived in full force. And after spending the better part of the morning in her small kitchen, nearly baking herself alongside her zucchini muffins she had decided to make at the last minute for the county fair's bake-off, the last thing she needed was to continue cooking in a dysfunctional hunk of metal. Again, Sara swore she would never wait until the last minute. Again, she believed herself.

Why didn't she listen to her father, her brother, or for that matter anyone, when they'd tried to explain how to fix a flat tire? Her sixteen-year-old daughter knew how to fix the darn thing, and she didn't even drive yet. I'm pathetic, she thought to herself.

As she smoldered on that country road, the only sound Sara heard, save the chirping of a way-too-happy bird, was the growl of protest from her stomach. She'd been so busy trying to get the muffins to the contest on time that she hadn't eaten breakfast.

"Fine," she said out loud to herself. "Maybe I can't fix some stupid, old car tire, but I can bake the best zucchini muffins in the county." Sara reached for the muffin box on the back seat and grabbed one. She took a bite, trying to soothe her bruised ego and ravenous hunger in one fell swoop. Blue ribbon, without a doubt, she thought, as she quickly gobbled the rest of the muffin down.

Sara felt a little better having eaten the muffin, but she was still stuck at the side of the road with no tow truck in sight, and the car was starting to warm up like an oven. She laid her head back against the car seat's headrest and tried to relax as she looked out at the row upon row of farmland that spread out before her. Why can't there be just one plowboy out there to ride up on his trusty tractor and save this damsel in distress? She closed her eyes and sighed heavily. It had been one heck of a morning.

"Howdy, Ma'am," drawled out a smooth voice.

Sara opened her eyes and turned her head in the direction of the voice. Standing beside her car leaning into the window on the driver's side was an extremely handsome man—his six-foot frame totally blocked the hot sun. He wore faded jeans that molded to his body, leaving little to the imagination. His sleeveless shirt, unbuttoned from the heat, allowed Sara to see that underneath was nothing but lean, hard muscle. From the

14

top of his straw hat to the heels of his boots, this man was pure stud. If he had any flaws, Sara couldn't see them. She ran her tongue across her parched lips as her eyes took in this candidate for an All-American poster boy. If Sara thought it was hot before, now it was sizzling.

He tipped back his straw hat and gave her a brilliant smile. "Looks like you need some help. Name's Beau. What can I do for you?"

Many, many ideas raced through her mind, and none of them had anything to do with a broken-down car or a box full of muffins.

Sara managed to get out of the car and point, rather clumsily, at the tire. "Flat. No jack. Tow truck coming," she sputtered.

"Well," he said with his cute Southern accent, "reckon we'll just have to find something to do while we wait."

Beau took her hand and led her out into the field between two rows of low bushes. She didn't ask where he was taking her. She was his for the taking. Stopping, he squatted down and motioned her to follow. Again, Sara didn't hesitate.

Now, close to the earth, Sara took in its heady, rich smell. She never realized how intoxicating dirt could be, but then again, she'd never been down in the dirt with a hunky farmer before. He took her hand and guided it into the bush, past the large green leaves. Her hand immediately found the firm, long squash, and she gasped a little in surprise.

"Go on. Pick it," Beau said.

She gave a gentle tug and it detached easily. Pulling it from the bush, she found a perfect, dark green zucchini in her hand.

"Beautiful . . . ," Beau's voice trailed off.

"Yes, this is a lovely zucchini," agreed Sara, still staring at it.

"No," said Beau, gently pulling her chin so she faced him. He looked her straight in her eyes and said softly, "I was talking about you."

Sara stood there speechless, still holding the zucchini. Okay, okay, her mind raced. She took a big, gulping breath. I'm obviously delusional now. I must have worked too hard in the heat.

Beau ran a finger down the side of her face. Sara shivered from the heat of his caress and let a small sigh escape her lips. Beau gave her a sultry smile. He knew what he was doing to her, and he knew he was doing it well. Obviously, all that time working with his hands had paid off in a big way.

As his caress continued down to her shoulder, Sara leaned into it. She savored his touch, which was strong and yet so gentle.

"You know, there's nothing I like better than planting my seeds in fresh, fertile ground," he crooned, giving her a sensuous smile and a wink. He took her in his arms and pulled her close. "Mmm, mmm . . . nice and ripe."

Sara's breath caught. She wanted to tell him he could plow her field any time. She wanted to tell

16

him she'd gladly drive his tractor. She wanted to tell him—

Honk! Honk!

A horn bellowed from behind Sara's car. Sara bolted up; her back ramrod straight. Looking in her rearview mirror, she saw a fat, stubble-faced, short, middle-aged mechanic step out of his tow truck. "Hey, lady," he called with teeth clenched tightly to his cigar, "you the broad that needs her tire changed?"

Sara just stared, not quite out of her stupor. There, in a split second, went all of her pretty dream—poof!—gone with the sound of the seedy mechanic's gravelly voice.

"It took you long enough!" Sara reeled. "Spare's in the trunk."

"Sorry!" he snapped back, not at all contrite. As he headed for her trunk, he shook his head and mumbled under his breath. "Dumb broad takes it out on me 'cause she can't fix her own freakin' tire."

Sara shoved another zucchini muffin in her mouth to keep from speaking her mind and possibly winning a blue ribbon for Best Expletive. With any luck, she still might make it to the fair in time for the judging. Even if I don't, she thought with a smile, I'll have all of my zucchini muffins left over. People had always told her they were special. Maybe, just maybe, they could work their special magic on her again. It could happen, right?

The grungy mechanic looked at Sara sitting in her car with that odd smile on her face and asked, "You okay, lady? Don't pass out on me or nothin', 'cause I ain't no doctor."

Sara turned to him and said sweetly, "I'm perfectly fine. I have something important I need to check into, so could you please hurry and fix the tire?"

He eyed her sideways. "You ain't one of them bi-polars, are ya? 'Cause I seen a program on TV . . . " he began.

"Just fix the tire," Sara repeated. She then began to hum to herself.

When the mechanic was done, Sara waved goodbye and drove off. The mechanic scratched his bristly chin and watched her drive out of sight. "Nutty broad oughta learn how to fix a tire," he muttered.

17

zzzzzesty muffins

makes 14–16 muffins

1 cup flour

½ cup yellow cornmeal

2 teaspoons baking powder

¼ teaspoon salt

½ cup butter, melted

½ cup sugar

2 eggs, beaten

1 can (15 ounces) black beans, drained

1 cup mild salsa

2 cups cooked chicken, finely chopped

1 can (7 ounces) chopped green chiles, drained

¼ cup finely chopped onion

¼ cup shredded jack cheese

¼ cup shredded cheddar cheese

1. Preheat oven to 350 degrees.

2. In a large bowl, mix together dry ingredients (flour through salt). Form a well in the center. Set aside.

3. In a separate bowl, mix together butter, sugar, and eggs. Fold in black beans, salsa, chicken, chiles, onion, and cheeses until just blended. Pour into dry-ingredient well and stir until just moistened.

4. Lightly grease or paper-line muffin cups. Fill each cup ¾ full with batter. Bake 20 to 25 minutes or until a toothpick comes out clean. Cool 5 minutes before removing from pan.

18

if you like zzzzzesty muffins, then you'll love

Armando

In the cover of night, he comes—a man of secrets and intrigue. Your Latin lover's black cape and tight leather pants only partly hide the incredibly defined, lithe body. Olé! Armando's piercing coal eyes—framed by his mysterious dark mask—meet yours for a fleeting moment, and that's all it takes to make the sultry night even hotter. In an instant, he's gone, but at your door he leaves behind a muffin with a smoldering Z branded on the top. A guilty smile creeps across your face. You know he'll be back.

tally me banana muffins

makes 12 muffins

1. Preheat oven to 350 degrees.

2. In a large bowl, mix together dry ingredients (flour through sugar). Form a well in the center. Set aside.

3. In a separate bowl, stir together bananas, butter, eggs, and sour cream. Pour into dry-ingredient well and stir until just moistened. Fold in walnuts.

4. Lightly grease or paper-line muffin cups. Fill each cup ¾ full with batter. Bake 20 to 25 minutes or until a toothpick comes out clean. Cool 5 minutes before removing from pan.

1½ cups flour

1 teaspoon baking soda

½ teaspoon salt

1 cup sugar

3 medium ripe bananas, mashed

½ cup salted butter, melted

2 eggs, beaten

¼ cup sour cream

½ cup chopped walnuts

21

Going Bananas

Kate had been slaving for weeks over a project report for her boss. Evenings, weekends, and lunch hours found her working feverishly. She hoped that maybe, just maybe, this would be the project that would get her the advancement she needed to move up. She worked up to the last second, making quick changes and improvements until it was absolutely perfect. Holding her breath, Kate gave it to her boss for final approval for the next day's meeting with the bigwigs.

When she entered the boardroom already filled with suits, she saw her report in front of each seat. Nervously, she sat down and looked at the covered and bound stack of papers that represented the last two months of her life. But she almost screamed out loud when she looked at the bottom. There, instead of her name, was blazed the name of her boss. Incredulous, she caught his eye, and he gave her a look that said, "What are you going to do about it?" Kate instantly knew what she was going to do. She stood, turned, and walked out the door, purse in hand. She quit.

In the heat of the moment, she did yet another impulsive thing. She called her travel agent friend. "Book me a vacation. I don't care where, but I want to leave tomorrow." Within twenty-four hours, Kate found herself landing at Montego Bay Airport in Jamaica.

As she stepped off the plane, two things hit her. First, she couldn't believe she had quit her job and was now standing in paradise. She looked around and her eyes almost couldn't comprehend how gorgeous the island was. No picture could have done it justice.

The second thing to hit her was the humidity. It had to be ninety degrees and ninety percent humidity, and Kate realized she had the wrong clothes. She made a mental note to do some shopping once she checked in to her hotel.

However, the next two hours on the island made Kate fearful she'd never make it to the hotel. She had made the unfortunate choice of hailing the cab of a very disgruntled driver, one with possible suicidal tendencies. Before she was barely seated in the back, he revved the engine, lurched into first gear, and cranked up a Harry Belafonte CD, the latter probably for the tourists' benefit. As the calypso rhythms of the Banana Boat Song blared in her ear, he barreled their tiny car through narrow streets and mountain roads. As Harry belted, "Come, mister tally man, tally me banana . . . ," Kate remembered thinking, Come, mister tally man, or mister policeman, or mister anybody and save me!

22

When the cab finally came to a screeching halt, Kate's nerves were still shot but her knuckles were finally beginning to loosen up and lose their whiteness. She had the urge to kiss the ground in gratitude, but with one look around, she quickly forgot her taxi ride from hell. What loomed before her was nothing short of heaven on earth. Never could she have dreamed up such paradise. Once checked in, she was led to an open, airy room with a larger veranda that overlooked the white sandy beaches and an ocean the color of sapphire. It was perfect. Everything was perfect, all except her heat-trapping wardrobe. She returned to the front desk to ask for the nearest shopping spot.

"That is in Ocho Rios," said the male receptionist in a beautiful Jamaican voice. "About ten miles south."

She was hoping it was in walking distance. "I have to take another cab ride?" she asked weakly. The receptionist could sense the trepidation in her voice.

"You didn't care for our taxis, Ma'am?" he said with a knowing smile. She shook her head violently. "I will have Rico take you then," he replied. He turned toward the back room. "Rico!"

"Oh, no, there's no need," she began, not wanting to put anyone out. "I can take a . . ." She stopped midsentence. She couldn't talk anymore because there, before her, was a man who literally took her breath away. Every feature was like it had been painted on by the most talented artist in the world. From his coal-black eyes, to his nose, to his full lips which framed his sparkling smile, he was a masterpiece. He wore a thin white cotton shirt and tan linen pants that fit him very well, accentuating his lean, muscular frame. Kate now desperately needed those cooler clothes, because it was getting hot, hot, hot in there!

Every feature was like it had been painted on by the most talented artist in the world.

"Rico, please take this young lady to Ocho Rios to shop," said the man. Rico gave Kate a quick smile. "Yes, sir." He walked around the desk and offered his arm, leading her out the door.

Kate still hadn't said much as they got in a very small car. As Rico started the engine, she found her voice. "You're not a crazy driver, too, are you?"

He chuckled as he put the car in first gear and carefully, slowly pulled away from the hotel. "No,

23

miss," he replied. "I'll keep you safe." And Kate did feel safe with him, even in that tiny tin box of a car.

They drove in silence, giving Kate a chance to look around. It was stunningly beautiful. Everything seemed to be the most intense shades of blues, greens, and whites, like it was all colored with brand-new crayons. But the beauty of the landscape couldn't compare to the beauty of her driver, of whom she kept stealing glances. It was like he was a magnet for her eye. She couldn't stop looking at the gorgeous island eye candy next to her.

Suddenly, Kate yelled, "Pull over!" Rico quickly did, and turned to her with concern in his eyes. "Miss, are you all right?"

"Bananas! On a tree!" she exclaimed, pointing to a plant just on the side of the road. Rico smiled at her excitement and got out of the car. He began softly whistling the Banana Boat Song she had heard in the cab as he walked over to the plant and pulled off a large, perfect banana. As she watched him closely in the light of the tropical sun, she found herself softly singing along, ". . . tally me banana. Daylight come and me wanna go home . . . " But Kate knew that she never wanted to go home. At that moment, she wanted to stay in paradise with her gorgeous tally man forever.

Rico returned, still whistling the tune, and she caught herself staring at his lips and enjoying how they puckered. He finished the song as he handed the banana to her. "An island gift."

She smiled back and took the fruit. She peeled back the bright yellow skin and took a bite. Never had she tasted something as good. She smiled at Rico. *Never has anyone looked so good,* she thought.

"If you like bananas, Miss, I can take you to a bakery in town where they make delicious banana muffins," he said.

"Do you take care of all your guests so well?" she asked, genuinely curious.

"Only the pretty ones," he said with a grin. "For you, I will make sure you are pleased."

As they drove off, slowly, she smiled and mentally began to tally all the many ways he could please her.

24

gingerbread man
muffins **makes about 12 muffins**

2½ cups flour

½ cup sugar

1½ teaspoons baking soda

1 teaspoon cinnamon

1 teaspoon ground ginger

½ teaspoon ground nutmeg

1 cup dark molasses

1 cup buttermilk

½ cup salted butter, melted

1 egg, slightly beaten

1 cup walnuts, chopped

Whipped cream for garnish

1. Preheat oven to 350 degrees.

2. In a large bowl, mix together dry ingredients (flour through nutmeg). Form a well in the center. Set aside.

3. In a separate bowl, mix together molasses, buttermilk, butter, and egg. Pour into dry-ingredient well and stir until just moistened. Fold in walnuts.

4. Lightly grease or paper-line muffin cups. Fill each cup ¾ full of batter. Bake 15 to 20 minutes, or until toothpick inserted in center comes out clean. Cool 5 minutes before removing from pan.

5. Serve warm or cool with a dollop of whipped cream on the top.

26

if you like gingerbread man muffins, then you'll love

Gin

Do you know the Muffin Man? If you've never met this one, I can assure you that he is a feast for the eyes! Gin is a tall, handsome softy made of pure sweetness and just the right touch of spice. His warm demeanor will surely make your own temperature start to rise. What would you do to catch this gingerbread man?

hot stuff muffins

makes 14 muffins

1 cup flour

¾ cup sugar

2 teaspoons baking powder

1 teaspoon baking soda

½ teaspoon salt

1 cup quick cooking oats

1 egg, beaten

3 tablespoons salted butter, melted

1¼ cups milk

⅔ cup hot pepper jelly

Topping:

2 tablespoons sugar

2 tablespoons flour

3 teaspoons cinnamon

1 teaspoon salted butter, melted

1. Preheat oven to 400 degrees.

2. In a large bowl, mix together dry ingredients (flour to oats). Form a well in center. Set aside.

3. In a separate bowl, whisk together egg, melted butter, milk, and jelly until smooth. Pour into dry-ingredient well and stir until just moistened.

4. Lightly grease or paper-line muffin cups. Fill each cup ¾ full with batter.

5. In a small bowl, mix together topping ingredients. Sprinkle evenly over batter. Bake 15 to 20 minutes or until a toothpick comes out clean. Cool 5 minutes before removing from pan.

28

if you like hot stuff muffins, then you'll love

Dante

It's getting hot, hot, hot—and Dante's soul burns for you. He may not be a real devil, but his devil-ish grin shows that he can be as naughty as you need him to be. Let him take you to an inferno of red-hot love that will melt your heart and bring out your deepest desires. He'll make you feel heat like you've never felt it before.

breakfast in bed muffins
makes 12 muffins

1. Preheat oven to 350 degrees.

2. In a skillet, fry sausage and bacon until sausage is browned and bacon is crisp. Drain on paper towels.

3. In a large bowl, mix together flour, baking powder, salt, and baking soda. Form a well in the center. Set aside.

4. In a separate bowl, stir together eggs, sour cream, and milk. Stir in bacon, sausage, cheese, onion, and green pepper. Pour into dry-ingredient well and stir until just moistened.

5. Lightly grease or paper-line muffin cups. Fill each cup ¾ full of batter. Bake 20 to 25 minutes, or until a toothpick comes out clean. Cool 5 minutes before removing from pan.

¼ pound bacon, diced

¼ pound bulk pork sausage

2¼ cups flour

3 teaspoons baking powder

½ teaspoon salt

½ teaspoon baking soda

2 eggs, slightly beaten

½ cup sour cream

²/₃ cup milk

1 cup grated cheddar cheese

¼ cup onion, diced

¼ cup green pepper, diced

A Very Good Morning, Indeed

Monique hated it when it happened: twenty minutes before the alarm was to go off, something would wake her up. Sometimes it was the trash truck; she swore the drivers intentionally dropped their bins from the greatest possible height. She had known this would present a problem when she and her husband rented that apartment with an alley behind. Other times it was the maniacal screeching of the neighbor's parrots in the building directly across from their bedroom window; was there such a thing as bird psychosis medication? Once in a while she would be able to drop back off to sleep, but usually her brain kicked into gear, ticking off all of the things on her day's agenda. And once that list began, there was no turning back.

This morning's early wakeup call was Sparky, who had stealthily crept to the side of her bed, then pounced directly on top of Monique, like a puma in a sixty-pound Labrador retriever costume. He clumsily climbed over her to the center of the bed, planting his feet against her and pushing until his back wedged against her husband, then immediately settled into the sleep of the puppy angels.

Her husband, who had been known to sleep through earthquakes, didn't break the cadence of his buzz-saw snore, while Sparky broke into his own snore pattern that was distinctly dissonant from her husband's. Monique stared in disbelief at the scene in her bed, dramatically threw the pillow over her head, and tried desperately to will herself back to sleep.

Pack the kids' lunches . . . throw in a load of laundry . . . GO BACK TO SLEEP . . . find good pair of nylons (or at least one where the holes are above hem line), get gas . . . STOP IT! Tick, tick, tick. She turned away from the din next to her and tried to pull on the faded blue comforter, only to find it firmly stuck under her bedmates. Partially covering herself with the three inches of comforter they had left her, she tried, once again, to reclaim her sleep. However, the litany in her head started up again.

Give the landlord the rent check . . . take Sparky for a walk . . . OH, PLEASE! . . . remember to e-mail conference schedule . . . fix breakfast . . . NO! NO! NO!

Monique pulled the pillow tighter to her face. "Great, now I'm awake and hungry," she quietly mumbled into it. She sat up briefly and stared at the clock,

32

willing it to stop—or at least slow down—and then flopped over and buried her head under the pillow again. It was cruel and unusual punishment.

"Pssst, Monique...Are you up, yet?" came a muffled voice from behind the bedroom door.

She immediately froze. Slowly, she pulled the pillow down. Soft morning light washed over the room, giving it an ethereal aura. She looked around and found she was alone in her bed. Gone were her snoring bedfellows. Looking down, she found that her faded blue comforter was replaced by a thick white eiderdown quilt made from the finest satin. Looking under it, she saw that her husband's T-shirt and boxers she wore as pajamas were also gone, replaced by . . . nothing. She quickly pulled the quilt closer around her, a little rattled but still reveling in the unbelievable softness of it against her bare skin. What was going on?

She almost forgot what woke her up when she saw the door open slowly. Despite the warmth of the quilt, she felt a chill run down to her toes, for there, nearly filling the frame of the doorway, stood Gianni—six-foot-two, freshly showered, and more handsome than one man should be allowed to be. He wore blue pajama bottoms that sat low on his hips and a white robe that fell slightly from his shoulders. In his hands was a white breakfast tray that carried a glass of juice, a rose, and a perfect breakfast muffin.

"It's about time, sleepyhead," he chuckled softly as he approached her bed. Okay, she thought, this the best dream ever. If those parrots wake me up now, I'm going to be in trouble with the Society for the Prevention of Cruelty to Animals.

Gianni placed the tray in the middle of the bed and then slowly climbed in. Stretching out next to it, he propped his head up in his hand and gave her a sultry grin. He picked up the rose, letting the petals slowly caress his lips.

"Thought you might be hungry," he said with a sly grin. "I know I am."

He rose to his knees and picked up the tray, then placed it over her lap. In one smooth movement, he swung his leg over and straddled her, gently but firmly pinning her deeper into the bed. Without a word, he held the muffin to her lips, and she took a bite. Sausage, peppers, and bacon—it was incredible. She just loved bacon.

"Take another bite," he said seductively. "You'll need your strength."

She did as she was told, staring directly into his dark eyes, afraid to blink for fear he would disappear.

"You know," he said playfully, "we don't have to leave this bed, if we don't want to. C'mon . . . Let's play hooky today. Wanna?"

Monique nodded enthusiastically. Oh, the things she wanted to play with him. A new litany filled her

33

head, but some of the items on the list even made her blush. But her reality-based brain kicked back in. "No, I can't. I've got a meeting, and the kids have to go to the orthodontist at four, and Sparky needs a walk—"

She watched as each muscle flexed and defined. Her morning kept getting better by the minute.

He gently placed his fingertips over her lips. She stopped talking, thoroughly enjoying the sensation of his soft touch on her lips. "No, you don't."

She started to protest again, but this time he silenced her lips with a kiss. It was soft and firm at the same time, and she felt her toes curl. When he pulled back, he gave her a devious smile. "You were saying?"

Monique felt her brain go to mush, and all of the lists and errands and meetings evaporated from her mind like the steam from the manholes outside the apartment. "I . . . have no idea," she said, breathlessly.

Gianni looked at her, staring deeply into her eyes.

Monique stared back, as if caught by some magical, mesmerizing tractor beam. She had never seen such a beautiful face on such a beautiful man. She suddenly had no problem turning off the constant barrage of thoughts that ricocheted in her brain. Gianni was all she needed to see, to know, to hear. He was her everything, and she was going to be just fine living the rest of her life in that bed.

He lifted himself from the bed and stretched lazily. She watched as each muscle flexed and defined. Her morning kept getting better by the minute. She continued watching as he walked to the window. "I need to see you better," he said as he began pulling on the curtain.

"You won't get much light from that window, because the building next door—" her voice cut off, mid-sentence. When Gianni opened the curtains all the way, gone was the ugly gray building that was almost within an arm's reach. What she saw out her crystal-clear window was a vast field of daisies, all yellow and white, as far as the eye could see. The morning sun glinted off the dew on their petals, making the entire ground look like a glittery wonderland. Beautiful (and silent!) birds fluttered by, while a small herd of curious deer grazed nearby. Monique looked at Gianni with utter shock. He just smiled again and climbed back into bed next to her.

34

"What would you like for the next course?" he breathed. He moved in closer and began nibbling on her ear. Or was he licking . . . ?

Monique opened her eyes and found Sparky lazily slobbering on the side of her face, his tail thumping against the bed. She sat up with a start and pulled her three inches of faded blue bedspread up to wipe her slimy face.

"Get down, Sparky!" she snapped as she shoved the dog to the ground. Her dream! She quickly closed her eyes. Maybe it would come back, if she tried really hard. She pulled the pillow over her face again and began chanting in her head: Sleep, sleep, oh, come on, SLEEP!

Slowly, she sat up and pulled the covers back down, first opening one eye, then the other. Did it work? Was he back? But one look around the room told her he wasn't. All she saw was her faded blue bedspread, a snoring husband, and a slobbery dog at the side of her bed. It was over. So over. With a huge, frustrated sigh, she plopped back down, staring at the ceiling, and trying not to cry.

Her husband stretched his arms out and turned his body around to face her while still keeping his eyes closed. "Everything okay?" he asked groggily.

"Yes," she muttered. Obviously, she couldn't tell him that she was upset because her fantasy man was no longer in their bed. Husbands just didn't understand these things.

He sat up and rubbed his head. "I'm kind of hungry. Do you know if we have any cereal left?"

"Actually . . . " she said, a little too emphatically, "we're going to have breakfast muffins this morning." Her man might be gone, but no one was going to take her bacon from her. No one.

35

five-alarm corn muffins

makes 12–15 muffins

1 cup flour

1 cup cornmeal

1½ teaspoons baking powder

1½ teaspoons baking soda

1 tablespoon chili powder

2 eggs, slightly beaten

1 cup frozen corn, thawed

½ cup mayonnaise

½ cup salted butter, melted

½ cup milk

1 can (4 ounces) chopped green chiles, drained

3 tablespoons hot pepper jelly

1 cup shredded pepper jack cheese

1. Preheat oven to 350 degrees.

2. In a large bowl, mix together dry ingredients (flour through chili powder). Form a well in the center. Set aside.

3. In a separate bowl, stir together remaining ingredients until blended. Pour into dry-ingredient well and stir until just moistened.

4. Lightly grease or paper-line muffin cups. Fill each cup ¾ full. Bake 15 to 20 minutes, or until a toothpick comes out clean.

36

Trey

Trey is a fireman and man on fire. He'll make your temperature rise as he heats things up to 350 degrees in your kitchen with a love that's almost too hot to handle. He has a flame in his heart that only you can extinguish. The friction created from your bodies will combust into an inferno of passion. He's ready to melt in your arms.

secret center muffins

makes 12 muffins

1. Preheat oven to 375 degrees.

2. In a large bowl, mix together dry ingredients (flour through salt). Form a well in the center. Set aside.

3. In a separate bowl, mix together eggs, milk, and butter. Pour into dry-ingredient well and stir until just moistened.

4. Light grease or paper-line muffin cups. Fill each cup ⅓ full of batter. Carefully spoon 1 teaspoon jam into center of each cup. Top with batter until cup is ⅔ full.

5. Bake 15 to 20 minutes, or until a toothpick comes out clean. Cool 5 minutes before removing from pan.

1¾ cups flour

½ cup sugar

1 tablespoon baking powder

½ teaspoon salt

2 eggs, beaten

⅔ cup milk

⅓ cup salted butter, melted

½ cup strawberry jam

39

Telling Secrets

Henri was one of my best operatives. He was well trained, discreet, and always the professional. Sadly, due to the sensitive nature of our business, we were never to meet in person. It was much safer that way. Our only contact was by phone or cryptic messages delivered covertly by an anonymous messenger. He knew me by my code name only: Muffin.

Yes, I know that sounded a little silly, but it was chosen in case our calls were ever tapped. That way it would appear he was merely talking to his lover, using a cute little pet name. Secretly, I adored it each time he called me that. Of course, I refrained from telling him how I felt, remembering the first rule of the Secret Agent: It's a secret.

Although he didn't know my face, I most certainly knew his. I knew every inch of that rugged profile, from those incredible blue eyes to the sharp edge of his jaw. I knew the curve of his lips, and how his left eyebrow would arch when he smiled. While he was spying on the evil forces of the world, I kept myself busy spying on him. He never knew my obsession, which, I guess made me the better spy. Not that we spies keep score.

His latest assignment was an odd one as it originated from an even more secretive department than mine. Even I didn't exactly who initiated the mission. I received sealed papers, directing him to a glamorous casino on the Italian Riviera. There, he was to track the laundering of terrorist money by an eastern European king. As it turned out, he not only had a license to kill, but also one to bake, so I placed him as a pastry chef inside the casino's three-Michelin-star restaurant. It was the perfect cover. He knew his meringue from his fondant. This would allow him to get close enough to King Sergei at his intimate dinner parties to eavesdrop on his conversations.

I arranged for Henri to rendezvous with another operative at the train depot with the documents he would need. Dressed like a common passenger, I hid in the shadows, watching him from afar as he stood against a depot pillar, looking nonchalant in his tuxedo. I watched as he deftly assessed his surroundings like the well-trained spy he was. He, as well as I, knew that any one of the passengers—either departing the train or waiting for the next arrival—could be a potential threat. Nothing slipped his notice; not the large gentleman eating the apple strudel made with lots of real butter and Macintosh apples that were probably overripe, or the woman in the designer suit with a small dark stain on the lower edge of her skirt, most likely from the packaged fudge

40

brownie she purchased from the vending machine in the lobby, nor the little girl with chocolate cookie crumbs all around her mouth—Hydrox, not Oreo. The man knew his dessert stains.

The operative showed promptly at six o'clock. Sidling up to Henri, he slipped the dossier he needed into his silver attaché case, slicker than a greased cake pan. Without a word, he was gone. Henri was then able to retrieve the file, unnoticed by the swarming crowd on the platform. I watched him read it, knowing that his photographic mind was hard at work. I loved how his brow furrowed when he was memorizing top-secret information.

According to the dossier, King Sergei and his entourage would be arriving at the restaurant at nine sharp for an evening of baccarat and fine dining. According to the report, it was thought that tonight was the night the king would be winning big so that he could funnel money to his terrorist organizations. Henri's mission was to find a way inside Sergei's secret circle. Oh, how I wish he would find his way inside my secret.

As Henri replaced the dossier, the six-thirty train pulled into the station. He stayed and watched who got off the train. As I said, you never know when you might come across a potential threat. And he lived for potential threats. The people began disembarking, and he gave each the once-over. As I watched him standing there, all suave and debonair, I was finding it difficult to stay away. I found myself drawn to him, like clarified butter. Maybe, just this once, I could walk by. It would put me closer than I'd ever been, but even that would be a risky move. I waited for a crowd to pass, and I joined in.

I was walking right at him. Then, quite unexpectedly, he looked directly at me. I felt my heart skip a beat, and it took all my effort to remember the training I had in spy school to look indifferent in the face of fear. And I feared I'd run right to his arms and hold on like tomorrow never came. Stay stoic, I chanted in my brain.

I was now a mere meter or two from him. His gaze never wavered. I tried not to return it, but it was as if he held some power over me. My pace unintentionally slowed a bit, and my brain raced as I tried to decide my next move. Do I stop? Do we speak? Could I take that chance? To my relief, the blast of the locomotive's whistle diffused the tension of the moment. Henri looked toward the train, and suddenly his attention diverted. He looked past me with such intensity that I wondered if he'd spotted an international villain.

I turned to catch a glimpse of what he was looking at and there before us was a woman so lovely that I saw Henri give her the once-over, twice. I could tell she came from money, as her clothes were impeccable and expensive. She had on large dark glasses and a huge brimmed hat that she obviously wore to be noticed, but not seen. Yet, even behind her veiled disguise, it was clear that she was stunning. Henri took a step toward her, but stopped short when he noticed the man following her was none other than King Sergei, who was now surrounded by his bodyguards. Was she his queen? I didn't recall any file making mention of her. Henri stepped back into the shadows of the depot and watched them pass. I continued to watch him as a sudden pang of jealousy swept through me.

I told myself to calm down, that he wasn't a monk, and he had every right to look at a beautiful woman. I also prayed that she was married to the king, although that never stopped him before.

Henri slipped out of the depot and into his sports car. I discreetly followed him to the casino, where he quickly changed into his chef's uniform. I took a table in a dark corner near the kitchen where I could see him in glimpses through the opening and closing door. My, he looks good in a chef's uniform, too, I thought.

I truly shouldn't have been there. I was jeopardizing the mission, but I couldn't help myself. I'm just conducting an employee observation, I justified in my mind. My professional evaluation? Yummy.

I could hear the kitchen buzzing with excited conversation about the king's arrival. It wasn't long before word spread that his party had just entered. Henri peered through the doors that separated the kitchen from the dining room, and I watched his eyes beeline to her again. Arm in arm with the king, she was wearing a sparkling dark blue Dior evening gown that revealed curvaceous hips, luscious breasts, and complemented her light green eyes and raven hair. The whole dining room had fallen silent when she entered. She looked even more amazing than she did at the depot, which didn't make me happy. Was that a smile on Henri's face? All right, I wasn't a little bit jealous, I was a lot bit jealous.

Once seated, King Sergei's party was served a sumptuous first course of salmon tartare on green olive crostini. After the army of first-class servers cleared the table, the second course of barbecued goose breast with an apricot vinaigrette was served. When the exquisite meal was finished, the king called for the maître d'.

"I would like to see the pastry chef, please," King Sergei said without looking up.

"Of course, Your Highness," replied the maître d' without hesitation. He waved Henri out. He breezed past me as he left the kitchen. This was officially the closest I'd ever been to him, and I learned something that can't come from a photo: he smelled incredibly good.

I watched him approach the king's table. Normally, he was one cool and collected secret agent. I had yet to see much that could get him worked up. I'd seen him in high-speed car chases, diffusing nuclear warheads, and dangling precariously by the ankles over toxic waste pits while double agents tried to procure his secrets, all without ever breaking a sweat. But tonight, I believe I saw him sweating a bit. I just prayed it was really hot in the kitchen, and it had nothing to do with the gorgeous woman in front of him.

Arriving at the king's table, I heard him ask, "How may I serve you, Your Highness?" He shot the woman a

42

quick glance. Was she smiling at him? And if she was, that was quite the seductive smile. That little vixen! Henri quickly glanced back to the king.

"I've heard that you are especially trained in American cuisine," said the king. "I would like you to prepare us a uniquely American dessert while we game at the baccarat table. I believe it is called Bananas Foster. I had it once when I was in New Orleans. Are you familiar with it?"

This would be the perfect dessert to make. It was, in fact, one of Henri's specialties, and its preparation would provide him the opportunity he needed to get close to the king's table.

"It would be my distinct pleasure to prepare it for you and the queen," he said. As the word "queen" left his lips, King Sergei arched his eyebrow slightly and looked at Henri inquisitively. Once again, Henri stole a glance at the queen. The smile was still on her lips, but now it looked a little more amused. I saw the look of confusion on Henri's face as he returned to the kitchen.

After the king and his party retired to the baccarat gaming room, I could see Henri begin to assemble his ingredients for the tableside preparation of the dessert. As he placed them on the stainless steel cart, I had a moment to reflect on the queen's amused look. *Did he say something humorous?* I don't think so, unless bananas made her laugh. The word is rather funny: ba-na-na. *Was his zipper down?* No, I had already checked his pants. I always made sure my operatives were properly dressed, of course.

Henri rolled his portable hot plate and skillet out to the gaming room and stood at attention next to the king, awaiting his command to begin the dessert presentation. I could only see his backside now, and I decided that looked proper, as well.

The king leaned over to the beauty at his side, brushed her glistening black hair back from her ear, and whispered, "You will love this dessert, my dear—just as much as my friends in the Middle East will enjoy the millions I have won at the tables tonight."

At the king's command, Henri caramelized the dark brown sugar in the rich cream butter. After adding the sliced bananas, he poured in the dark rum and banana liquor. Using a long match, he confidently lit the alcohol in a huge burst of flames. The show was a hit with the king's party, drawing cheers and loud applause. I silently wished he could light my fire.

After serving the king, queen, and the other guests, he stood at his station waiting to be dismissed. To my dismay, the queen turned to him and smiled again. "Your dessert was delicious," she said, a little too breathily.

"I am honored that you are pleased, Queen," he said.

"But you are mistaken, I am not the queen," she said, smiling but looking at him awkwardly. "I am Princess Natasha, the king's sister."

What? How could my case intelligence not have mentioned that the king had such a beautiful sister? This was an unfortunate turn of events, as Henri could get rid of brothers much more efficiently than husbands. I just

43

lamented that it was way too late to have sent a different operative.

"I apologize for the mistake, Your Highness," I heard him say, with just a bit too much enthusiasm.

"No harm was done," the princess replied, coyly. She thrust out her delicate hand and said, "It was my pleasure to have tasted your work."

Even from my vantage point, I could see her clumsily pass him a note when he accepted her hand. What an amateur, I thought. Henri can't be that impressed.

Henri stood back at attention until the king waived dismissively at him, then quickly returned to the kitchen. I crept to the door and watched as he opened the note with slightly trembling hands. What happened to that reserved spy? Could a beautiful woman truly undo years of extensive training that easily? I quickly pulled out my lipstick with the ocular zoom feature. I read the note along with him: My suite, Royal Plaza Hotel. Midnight. That hussy. She was not going to get my spy if I had anything to do with it. I hurried from the casino and into the sultry summer night.

I heard his knock on the door, and my heart raced. "Come in . . . . " I called from the shadows of the hotel room. I watched him step in and set down his silver attaché case, squinting to adjust to the darkened room. He had changed from his chef's uniform to one of his everyday tuxedos, and he looked so suave that my breath caught.

Before he had a chance to see clearly, I did what I've always secretly wanted to do: I pounced. I put my arms around his broad shoulders and embraced him with a deep, passionate kiss. I was so thankful when he returned my kiss in a way that was unmistakable. I didn't even care that he thought I was another woman. For that moment, I was his, and he was mine.

Suddenly, he scooped me up in his arms. I buried my head in his neck so he couldn't see my face as he carried me to the bed. I had only seconds to figure out what I was going to say, what I was going to do. But I couldn't concentrate, because his neck smelled so good. Foiled by his expensive cologne!

The moment of truth arrived as he lowered me onto the bed and we fell into each other's arms. I was ready for his shocked expression. I was ready for a barrage of questions. I was even ready for possible evasive action if he deemed me a threat. What I wasn't ready for was his smile, the one with the raised eyebrow I loved so much—or for what came out of his mouth.

"Hello, Muffin," he whispered playfully, amusement dripping in his voice.

For a moment, I was dumbfounded. "What . . . how . . . ?"

"I've got a secret for you," he said, still grinning. "You're not a good a spy as you think."

I still was having trouble comprehending what had just happened. He read the obvious confusion in my face. "I know who you are," he began. "I've known since the first day I started in Her Majesty's Service. And I know you bribed the bellhop with five hundred Euros to change the room numbers on the doors, so I'd come in here and not Princess Natasha's room."

44

"But . . . but it was supposed to be a secret!" I argued, relieved that he wasn't upset with my surprise.

"I'm a spy, remember?" he chuckled.

Strange, we were having this whole conversation with him still on top of me. It seemed perfectly natural, and perfectly wonderful.

"Aren't you worried the princess will be upset when you don't show?" I said, with a tone that was a tiny bit too jealous.

He leaned in closer, pressing his body closer to mine. The smile and raised eyebrow returned. "Muffin, there were no King Sergei and Princess Natasha. I set that up, knowing you were following me, knowing that you'd be here, tonight. Like I said, I know everything about you."

"Is that so?" I asked, trying not to sound flattered, but failing miserably. "Let's see about that. What's my favorite dessert, Mr. Pastry Chef?"

"Wait here," he said coyly, "I'll be right back." Henri quickly hopped off the bed and grabbed his attaché case, placing it on the bed. When he opened it and showed me it was empty, I gave him a puzzled look. "For your eyes, only," he said as he pressed a hidden button behind the handle. The false bottom in the case popped up, revealing a covered silver platter. Lifting the crisp white linen cover, he presented me with one of his handmade muffins.

I laughed with delight and reached for my favorite treat, but Henri teasingly slapped my hand. "What's the secret password?" he asked, trying to look dispassionate.

Then I gave him a kiss that would have broken any code ever created. Yes, he gave me the muffin. And I think I could have gotten him to divulge every secret Her Royal Majesty had entrusted him without much more effort.

I took a delicate bite of the muffin and my eyes grew wide when I discovered it held the secret center of thick fruit jam. "How did you know?"

"I just knew. Do you like it, Muffin?"

Of course, I did, but I didn't need to answer. He looked deep into my eyes, and he could tell that I did. He could always tell if someone was lying about baked goods.

"Now one last secret," he whispered into my ear. "Since the first moment we spoke, I knew that I wanted to go deep under cover with you, and only you. I am the spy who loves you. We can go away from here and start a new life together. We're booked on the midnight train, if you want to go."

My smile told him more than he had ever learned in Her Majesty's Service. He left me with one more passionate kiss and headed quickly for the door. "Meet me at the train station," he told me, as he opened the hotel door and checked the hallway.

"I'll be there, my love," I replied. Standing up, I went to go run a cold shower. All in a day's work, I mused to myself, taking the last bite of the decadent muffin. All in a day's work.

corny and sweet muffins   **makes about 12 muffins**

1½ cups flour

1 cup sugar

¾ cup cornmeal

1 tablespoon baking powder

½ teaspoon salt

1 egg

½ cup mayonnaise

⅓ cup salted butter, melted

1 cup milk

1. Preheat oven to 350 degrees.

2. In a large bowl, combine dry ingredients (flour through salt). Form a well in the center. Set aside.

3. In a separate bowl, mix together egg, mayonnaise, butter, and milk. Pour into dry-ingredient well and stir until just moistened.

4. Lightly grease or paper-line muffin cups. Fill each cup ¾ full of batter. Bake for 15 to 20 minutes, or until toothpick inserted in the center comes out clean. Cool 5 minutes before removing from pan.

46

if you like corny and sweet muffins, then you'll love

Lorenzo

Lorenzo is a man of many mysteries. He is known to some as telling cute, but corny jokes. He is also known as being sweet and debonair. He dresses with sophistication one day and then is sporting something relaxed and comfortable the next. His mysterious ways could write a novel. And that's just fine with us. Who doesn't like a good mystery?

high-stamina muffins makes 15 muffins

1½ cups whole wheat flour

1 cup quick cooking oats

1 teaspoon baking powder

1 teaspoon baking soda

½ teaspoon salt

1 teaspoon cinnamon

½ cup packed brown sugar

1 egg, beaten

¼ cup salted butter, melted

¼ cup honey

1¼ cups buttermilk

½ cup moist dates, pitted and chopped

½ cup chopped almonds

1. Preheat oven to 400 degrees.

2. In a large bowl, mix together dry ingredients (flour through brown sugar). Form a well in the center. Set aside.

3. In a separate bowl, stir together egg, butter, honey, buttermilk, dates, and almonds. Pour into dry-ingredient well and stir until just moistened.

4. Lightly grease or paper-line muffin cups. Fill each cup ¾ full of batter. Bake 15 to 20 minutes or until a toothpick comes out clean. Cool 5 minutes before removing from pan.

48

if you like high-stamina muffins, then you'll love

Jace

Ready, set, go! Jace will take you on a run you'll never forget. One look at his sleek and honed runner's body, and you can tell that he definitely has the stamina to go the distance. Jace will make your heart beat wildly with each step closer to that finish line. He's sure to win first place in your heart.

apple pie with cheddar muffins

makes about 12 muffins

1. Preheat oven to 375 degrees.

2. In a large bowl, mix together dry ingredients (flour through nutmeg). Form a well in the center. Set aside.

3. In a separate bowl, mix together egg, buttermilk, butter, and vanilla. Pour into dry-ingredient well and stir until just moistened. Fold in apples, cheese, and walnuts.

4. Lightly grease or paper-line muffin cups. Fill each cup ¾ full of batter. Bake 15 to 20 minutes or until a toothpick inserted in the center comes out clean. Cool 5 minutes before removing from pan.

2½ cups flour

⅓ cup sugar

1 tablespoon baking powder

½ teaspoon salt

½ teaspoon cinnamon

½ teaspoon ground nutmeg

1 egg, slightly beaten

1 cup buttermilk

⅓ cup salted butter, melted

1 teaspoon vanilla extract

2 cups chopped and peeled Granny Smith apples

½ cup sharp cheddar cheese, grated

½ cup walnuts, chopped

51

A New-Found Hope

Hope sat on the plane to Los Angeles, still a little overwhelmed that it was actually happening. Here she was, a small-town girl from North Dakota, on her way to a big city all alone. Two months ago, if someone would have told her she'd be doing this, she would have laughed at them. In fact, she would have thought it wasn't even a remote possibility, completely forgetting she had entered the baking contest months before. Life, as it has a way of doing, had taken over, and she relegated the contest entry to the far recesses of her brain.

Then one afternoon Hope got a call from her roommate, Becky, at the diner where she worked. She had to calm Becky down because she was talking way too fast and way too loud. "You did it! You made the top five! You're going to Los Angeles for a bake-off!" she screeched through the phone.

It became one of the biggest topics of conversation at the diner, and in fact the whole town. Within hours, people were coming in and calling, asking her about the contest and what she was going to make and what she was going to wear. She told them that it was a national baking contest sponsored by a flour company, and that she was going to be baking her famous (at least locally) Apple Pie with Cheddar Muffins—and that she had no idea what to wear.

Hope had worked at the diner, one of the few businesses in her tiny farming town of five thousand, since high school. Now, eight years later, she was the manager, and she loved her job. She enjoyed visiting with all of the customers—some she'd known all of her life—and she considered them more like family. But most of all, she loved that she had free rein in the kitchen to develop new recipes and try them out on the customers. She had to admit, she had definitely concocted her fair share of food creation duds, but most were amazing—and some even became permanent menù items.

It was during one of these experimental cooking sessions that she came up with the muffin concept. Actually, it was born from necessity—she had run out of apple pie, and she didn't have time to make a crust from scratch. In a moment of brainstorming clarity, she combined the apple pie ingredients with a simple muffin recipe. Then, on a whim, she threw in the cheddar cheese and baked it all together. What resulted was a delicious hybrid of pie and muffin that

52

quickly became a diner favorite that all the locals soon raved about.

Serendipity stepped into this story when Hope was making the muffins at home one day while a bored Becky sat at the counter and watched. As Hope measured and stirred, Becky picked up the bag of flour and read the announcement on the back for the baking contest.

"Hope! You can win one hundred thousand dollars!" she said. pointing at the bag of flour in disbelief.

"Sorry, I don't believe in sweepstakes," she said, not looking up and cracking an egg into the bowl.

"No," Becky said. "There's a baking contest. First prize is one hundred grand. Hope, you have to enter your muffins."

Hope knew the muffins were good, and she knew they were well worth the two dollars they cost at the diner. But she didn't know if they were worth a hundred thousand. "A million people enter those things," she said doubting herself.

"Yeah, but a million people can't make a muffin this good," Becky exclaimed, shrugging off the negativity. She quickly dipped her finger in the batter before Hope had a chance to smack it away. "So good!"

Curiosity made Hope pick up the flour bag and read the contest details. It did seem easy enough. All she had to do fill out an online entry form and attach a recipe that used their flour.

Becky stood behind her, looking over her shoulder as she read. "What have you got to lose?" she said, nudging her friend.

Hope thought for a second, and couldn't think of anything. "Okay, what the heck?" Becky let out a whoop and clicked on the computer. "You dictate, I'll type!"

They had the entry filled out and sent before the last muffin left the oven. Then, in all honesty, Hope forgot about it. That is, until she received the spastic call from Becky. From that moment on, it was all she could think about. She had a million things to do before she left for California—contact the contest's coordinator for information about the bake-off, send them a list of ingredients and utensils she'd need, research airfares, make arrangements at the diner for people to cover her shift, and so on.

Hope's excitement didn't diminish after the plane landed. She was whisked from the airport in a limo sent by the flour company (a definite first) to the five-star hotel that was hosting the competition. After checking in, she was shown her room—an incredible suite on the fifteenth floor with a view of the spectacular city below.

Next, she and the other contestants were to report to the main ballroom on the bottom floor. She considered changing into her new clothes, but she wanted to

53

apple pie with cheddar muffins

save them. For exactly what, she wasn't sure, but she figured she'd be dressed well enough for the tour of the kitchen with the other contestants. Besides, there weren't going to be pictures taken until tomorrow's competition.

Hope was the first to arrive at the ballroom. She entered the doorway and took a half-step inside, but then froze solid. In front of her was a sight she wasn't prepared for. Five complete kitchens had been set up, side by side, across the length of the ballroom. Each looked identical, and each looked like they were lifted from a picture she saw in those decorating magazines. There were stainless steel ovens and refrigerators, shiny black tabletop appliances, granite counters, and nested stacks of colorful mixing bowls and measuring tools. All she could do was stand there and try not to drool. It was a baker's nirvana, and it put her little kitchen in the diner to utter shame.

She had no idea how long she had been standing there when she heard a deep voice behind her. "Excuse me, but are you stuck?"

Shaken from her stupor, she quickly spun around. "I'm so sorry, but I can't believe—" Once again, she froze, but this time it wasn't the sight of the beautiful kitchen that she couldn't believe. It was the most beautiful hunk of man she had ever seen, standing less than two feet from her. He wasn't extremely tall, but he was certainly put together well. His shoulders were broad, accentuating his narrow waist, and it was obvious that he worked out, as his arms were toned,

rippled, and tanned. His strawberry blond hair and goatee were neat and trimmed, and the color of his hair made his green eyes just about pop from his head.

"Are you okay?" he asked, smiling at the dumbfounded look on her face.

"Oh, yeah," she said, a little too breathlessly. Why, oh why hadn't she changed her clothes? She pulled down on her T-shirt in a futile effort to cover the holes in her jeans.

He stood there, still smiling. She decided to smile back. He smiled bigger, then broke into a small laugh. "Is there any way I could get past you? Or are you the bouncer or something?"

"Oh!" she exclaimed and finally stepped aside to let him pass. Hope watched as he walked confidently up to one of the kitchens and opened the refrigerator, peering inside. She tried not to, but she couldn't help checking out his rear end when he bent over. It was a nice one. He looked up quickly and saw that she was staring. He gave her another bemused grin, and she looked away, blushing deeply.

Hope forced herself not to look back at him. Instead, she busied herself by filling out one of the nametags she found by the door. But she couldn't stop thinking about him. *He must be one of the company's representatives,* she guessed. If that were true, she would never buy another brand of flour as long as she lived. She smiled to herself.

Slowly, more people entered the room and began milling about. One of the other contestants introduced

54

herself to Hope, a stay-at-home mom from Montclair, California, named Jenny. They compared notes on how excited they were, but all the while, Hope kept Mr. Hot Buns in the corner of her eye. He was definitely heating up the kitchen, and no one had even turned on an oven yet. Finally, a rather plump woman went to the microphone and made an announcement.

"Welcome to the twenty-third annual Bake-Off Competition," she said to a round of applause. "Would all contestants please take a seat in this front row of chairs, and we'll get started with the orientation."

Hope and Jenny made their way toward the front and sat down. To Hope's utter surprise, Mr. Hot Buns walked in front of her and took the empty seat to her left. He's a contestant? Hope thought, incredulously. The thought had never even crossed her mind. How could someone who looks like him be a baker? she wondered. What kind of stuff did he make? Did he ever bake in the nude? She found herself blushing again. Oh, my gosh, why would I even think that?

Hope sat perfectly motionless, afraid her holey jeans might brush against his neatly pressed slacks. Just the nearness of his body to hers made her breathe erratically and she prayed he couldn't hear it or see it. She knew she should be listening to what the flour lady was saying, but she was having extreme difficulty concentrating for some reason. She swallowed hard and prayed that whatever was being said was also written in her packet.

Finally, after what seemed an eternity, the flour lady stopped talking. After another round of applause, everyone got up. Hope started to walk away, almost relieved to get away from Mr. Hot Buns when she heard his voice.

"Hey, good luck tomorrow," he said, looking at her and sounding sincere. She picked up a slight accent, but she couldn't quite place it. She liked it, though.

Hope turned back and saw his smiling face. It was such a very nice face. She smiled back. "Oh, thanks. Same to you . . . . "

"Logan. New Orleans," he said, pointing to his nametag. That's the accent, she thought.

"Hope. North Dakota," she said, pointing to hers.

"Well, Hope, North Dakota, I hope you do well." He took her hand and did something completely unexpected—he kissed it. And with that, he turned and walked out of the room. She was completely flustered, but not enough to stop her from watching him leave. Yes, those are some buns I'd like to knead, she thought, and once again, she blushed to her toes at the stuff her brain was coming up with.

Hope had trouble sleeping that night. She knew it was partly because of nerves for the contest but mostly because she couldn't wait to see Logan in the morning. She had never met anyone like him, especially not in North Dakota. Young, eligible men were few and far between back home. After tossing and turning

apple pie with cheddar muffins

55

in the most luxurious bed she'd ever had and trying desperately to get him out of her head, she finally fell into a fitful sleep.

In the morning, she tried to forget about Logan and concentrate on getting ready. She showered and put on the dress and jewelry Becky had helped her buy, and then fished the shoes from the bottom of her suitcase. They were pretty pumps with a two-inch heel—not high by any standard, but much higher than what she usually wore, especially to bake in. She got dressed, fixed her hair, and actually put on make-up, a rarity. Once done, she appraised herself in the mirror. "Not bad," she said aloud, "for a baker from North Dakota." Then she took a confident step toward the door and nearly fell off her shoes. "Balance, girl, balance!" she told herself.

She practiced walking in her heels in all the way to the elevator, then all the way to the ballroom. By the time she reached the door, she felt a little less shaky. She paused, took a deep breath, and then entered the room.

The place was a swirl of sound and motion. People with clipboards scampered every which way. Television crews busily set up cameras and wires. Television crews? Did she miss that part while she was busy drooling over Logan, New Orleans? She was now glad that she wore her nicer stuff.

Hope's eyes quickly scanned the room and she found her target. Logan was already busy in his little kitchen, preparing his things. He wore choco-late brown pants and a cream-colored shirt. He was also sporting a blue apron with the flour company's logo that all of the contestants would be wearing. He looked incredible, and she found herself staring, once again. She forced herself to look away and focus on the woman at the sign-in table by the door.

"You are assigned to kitchen three," she said, pointing to the one next to Logan. Hope's heart leapt, but then she quickly worried if this might make her baking suffer. How could she concentrate on muffin batter with a stud muffin within arm's reach? "Right now, you need to make sure all of your ingredients and implements are ready. Good luck!" Hope thanked her and picked up her apron. She took another deep breath and walked, now a little unsteady again, to her station. She hadn't quite reached it when Logan looked up and saw her.

"Good morning," he said, flashing his big, genuine smile. "You look very nice."

Her heart started pounding again. "Thanks," she self-consciously, then stepped up to her kitchen. On step two, she lost her balance and fell, landing with a thud.

Logan leapt over to her side. "Are you okay?" he asked, helping her back to her feet. No, I'm going to die from mortification, she thought, but managed a little nod.

She realized he was still holding her arm, and she felt like a thousand little bolts of electricity were shooting through her skin. They looked at each other

56

for a lingering moment before Logan broke the silence. "Be careful, now," he said with a devilish grin. "Baking's a dangerous profession." Stupid though she felt, Hope couldn't help but smile back.

Logan let go of her arm and returned to his kitchen. Hope tried to force herself to forget what had just happened, both the fall and the electricity, and to concentrate on the task at hand. First she assembled her bowls and measuring tools. That was one thing she liked about making muffins—they didn't need a lot of appliances, just a couple of bowls and spoons. She was glad she didn't need to use the mixer they had provided, which was a thing of beauty, all big and shiny. But the contraption had more buttons and gizmos on it than she had in her car, and she had to admit it intimidated her.

Next she had to make sure all the ingredients were there. She got out her list. Flour (of course), check. Butter, got it. Cheese, a nice cheddar. Hope caught a movement out of the corner of her eye. Not so covertly, she stole a glance at her hunky competitor. She watched as he arranged his ingredients on the counter. He looks good in a kitchen, she thought. He'd look better in my kitchen. Hope rolled her eyes and told herself to shut up.

Logan must have sensed Hope's stare because all of a sudden he looked over and smiled. He took a step toward her, leaning on his counter.

"So, would it break any rules if I asked you what you're making?" he asked.

"Apple Pie with Cheddar Muffins," she told him, trying to sound casual. "One of my creations. And you?"

"Mine's apple, too. I'm making Apple Beignets."

Hope had never heard that word before. "Beign-whats?"

Logan chuckled. "Beignets. They're like Cajun apple fritters, just with a lot more powdered sugar."

Hope was still a little confused as to what a beignet was, but if it had apples and powdered sugar, it couldn't be bad. "Sounds tasty."

She liked how his brow furrowed a bit as he worked. It made him look even cuter . . .

He took a step closer. "I'll make you a deal. Win or lose, we share our recipes after the competition. I'd love to taste what you make."

I'd love to taste you, said her brain. Blushing. More blushing. "It's a deal," she said, quickly looking away and hoping he didn't see her beet-red cheeks.

Suddenly, a voice boomed from the loud speaker. "Contestants, you have five minutes to competition. Please make any last-minute preparations."

Logan and Hope quickly returned to their work-stations. Hope tried to regain her focus, but as the last minutes ticked off, she found herself thinking only of Logan, covered in powdered sugar.

The flour woman from yesterday's meeting returned to the microphone and welcomed all to the competition. After a few brief notes, she readied the competitors. With a flourish, she dramatically counted down from ten, and the competition began.

Hope quickly got to work, starting with her dry ingredients. Although she knew this recipe like the back of her hand, she still checked and double-checked her printed directions, knowing that one error would result in disaster. Next, she mixed the butter, eggs, buttermilk, and sugar by hand and stirred them into the dry ingredients. All was going smoothly. Hope took a moment to steal a quick glance at Logan, who was using his monster mixer to blend something. She liked how his brow furrowed a bit as he worked. It made him look even cuter, if that was possible.

Hope turned her focus back to her muffins. It was time to pare the apples. But when she looked around, she didn't find any. Where were the apples? She ran to the refrigerator, but all that was in there was butter and eggs. She looked around frantically, opening all the cupboards and drawers in desperation. Where could they be? She quickly thought back. Hadn't she checked them off the list? Oh, no. She hadn't got that far when she stopped to talk to Logan. She didn't

have any apples! How could she make Apple Pie with Cheddar Muffins without apples? She was well on her way to a full-blown panic.

Her manic actions caught Logan's attention. Over the whir of his mixer, he called out, "Everything okay over there, North Dakota?"

Near tears, Hope shook her head. "I don't have any apples."

Logan turned off his mixer and walked over. "You sure?" he asked. She nodded, taking deep breaths to try and calm down.

Logan looked at her, then without a word, returned to his station. He picked up his apples and brought them to her. "Here," he said. "Use mine."

Hope couldn't believe what he was doing. He was sacrificing his apples for her. She shook her head violently. "Oh, no! I couldn't."

"Please, take them," he insisted. "I'll just make mine plain this time. They'll be Classic Beignets." He pressed the apples to her hands and gave her one of his famous, genuine smiles. "Really, it's fine."

Hope felt overwhelmed with emotion and began to cry anyway. "That's the sweetest thing—"

"No, my beignets are the sweetest thing, you'll see," he said, trying to lighten the mood. He took the towel from his pocket and dried her tears. "Don't cry; your batter will get salty. Now get back to work. Clock's ticking."

Somehow, Hope managed to finish her recipe, all the while amazed at what Logan had done for her. She

58

took a batch of perfect muffins from the oven and arranged them on a serving tray with a few minutes to spare, thanks to the kindness of a man who was beautiful both inside and out.

And then came time for the judging. The contestants brought their offerings to a long table in front of the judges. They all stood side by side, with Logan and Hope next to each other. Logan gave Hope a gentle nudge as the judges sampled her muffins. She gave him one back when they sampled his beignets.

Once the judges finished their scoring, the announcer lady called the contestants to the main stage. Logan stood close to Hope. She leaned over and whispered, "Thank you, again." He whispered back, "My pleasure," then added, "more than you know."

"This year's first-place prize recipe," the woman belted out, "and a check for one hundred thousand dollars is . . . "

She paused for a dramatic effect. Logan took Hope's hand in his. At that moment, she didn't care if she heard her recipe called or not. Hope knew she had just won a much better prize. ". . . the Chocolate Molten Cake!"

Jenny, the Montclair mom, shrieked and the room broke into wild applause. As the announcer handed the giant check to her, Logan leaned over and whispered seductively into Hope's ear. "I'm ready for your muffins. You ready for my beignets?"

Hope smiled and nodded. That, she decided, was not a half-baked idea.

59

taste of italy
muffins

makes about 12 muffins

2 cups flour

1 tablespoon baking powder

½ teaspoon salt

⅛ teaspoon garlic powder

3 tablespoon grated Parmesan cheese, divided

1 cup milk

¼ cup butter, melted

1 egg, slightly beaten

¼ cup prepared pesto sauce

1. Preheat oven to 375 degrees.

2. In a large bowl, mix together flour, baking powder, salt, garlic powder, and 2 tablespoons of the Parmesan cheese. Form a well in the center. Set aside.

3. In a separate bowl, mix together milk, butter, egg, and pesto sauce. Pour into dry-ingredient well and stir until just moistened.

4. Lightly grease or paper-line muffin cups. Fill each cup ¾ full of batter. Sprinkle remaining Parmesan cheese evenly over the batter. Bake for 20 to 25 minutes, or until a toothpick inserted in the center comes out clean. Cool 5 minutes before removing from pan.

Mario

When you look into Mario's dark brown eyes, you'll instantly want to sing "That's Amore." Let him help you take you on a fabulous ride down the romantic canals of Venice. Bada bing, bada boom—he's definitely a spicy taste of Italy that you will never forget!

wake me up muffins

makes 18 muffins

1. Preheat oven to 375 degrees.

2. In a large bowl, mix together dry ingredients (flour through salt). Form a well in the center. Set aside.

3. In a separate bowl, mix together milk, coffee granules, butter, egg, and vanilla extract until well blended. Pour into dry-ingredient well and stir until just moistened.

4. Fold in chocolate chips.

5. Lightly grease or paper-line muffin cups. Fill each cup ¾ full of batter.

6. To make streusel topping, combine flour, brown sugar, and cinnamon in a small bowl. Cut in butter using two forks or pastry blender until mixture crumbles. Sprinkle about a tablespoon of the mixture over each muffin.

7. Bake 15 to 20 minutes or until a toothpick comes out clean. Cool 5 minutes before removing from pan.

1½ cups flour

¾ cup sugar

1½ teaspoons baking powder

1½ teaspoons cinnamon

½ teaspoon salt

1 cup milk

3 tablespoons instant Suisse mocha coffee granules

½ cup salted butter, melted

1 egg, beaten

1 teaspoon vanilla extract

1 cup semisweet chocolate chips

Streusel Topping:

¼ cup flour

⅓ cup packed brown sugar

¼ teaspoon cinnamon

2 tablespoons cold salted butter

63

Rise and Shine

The alarm clock shrieked throughout the quiet of the house. Mattie cracked open one eye and was immediately assaulted by the bright, early spring sunshine. Rolling over to turn off the vulgar noise and catch some more zzzz's, she noticed the time was already forty minutes later than when she needed to be up. Evidently, she'd already had some extra sleep time and wasn't aware of it.

Groaning, she pulled herself out of bed, thinking this is what it must feel like to the people who claim "missing time" due to alien abduction. That would be an interesting story to tell people why I got fired today, she mused. Dragging her exhausted body to the bathroom, she appraised herself in the mirror. Her curly hair looked like a poodle after electroshock therapy, and her eyes had graduated from bags to suitcases. "Just lovely," she said to Punkin, her cat who sat on the sink, watching nonchalantly.

Quickly stripping down, Mattie turned on the shower and hopped in before the water had a chance to heat up. Her cry of protest, "OH . . . MY . . . GOD!" could be heard throughout the tristate area.

After a nanosecond shower, she climbed out, teeth chattering. Mattie wrapped herself in a large towel and grabbed her toothbrush. In an amazing feat of multitasking, she quickly brushed her teeth and dried off on the way to her closet, then threw on her sensible work suit, trying desperately to warm up. She put on one shoe and hopped back toward the bathroom as she put on the second.

In vain, she tried to comb her hair into a fashionable style, but quickly gave up and opted for the old standby: hair in a ponytail.

Bracing her hands on the edge of the sink, she looked at the image in the mirror. Punkin stood up and started rubbing against her arms, winding through them like a slalom course, purring at each turn. "You need a life . . . preferably one with a cute guy in it," she announced to herself. "You're young and you're living like a nun. Your late-night entertainment consists of the neighbors' dog, Buttons, who barks all night long. For gosh sakes, Mattie, the only male to enter your bedroom in the past three years has been your cat." She rubbed Punkin behind the ears, and he rewarded her with an extra-loud purr. "Pathetic," she said, shaking her head.

She grabbed her purse and keys off the nightstand and ran to the kitchen to grab a cup of coffee and the muffins she'd made for the potluck at work. Pulling

64

the tray of coffee and chocolate muffins out of the microwave where she'd hidden them from her carb-loving cat, she noted the neon clock on the coffee maker telling her she didn't have time to brew even a small pot before she had to go back to the real world as slave labor. I desperately need my coffee this morning after another night of Buttons's one-note concerto, she sighed to herself. Her mind raced, then reasoned: the muffins had her two favorite ingredients, and since both had caffeine, it could work, right? Her stomach rumbled in agreement.

Mattie grabbed a muffin she'd made off the tray and bit into it, letting its sweet, moist flavor fill her mouth. Closing her eyes, she said aloud, "I don't know if I'm more hungry or tired. Yum, simply . . . scrumptious."

"I agree," said a voice as smooth as a latte with extra-steamy milk.

Turning toward the voice, Mattie was greeted with a feast for her eyes. Leaning against the counter with a cup of coffee in his hand was a man who looked like he'd just walked out of a *GQ* magazine ad. From the cut of his suit to the polish of his shoe, there was no mistaking that this man was a total buck. The slight salt and pepper in his hair gave him an air of dignity. This was no office toady; this was executive ilk. He was the type of man who saw what he wanted and wouldn't stop until it was his. And he was looking at her.

Reality slipped back in and Mattie stammered, "Who . . . are you?"

A wide smile spread across his face, revealing perfect teeth. Then he raised his eyebrows and said innocently, "I'm Dalton, and as you can see, I'm not the cat, but if you stroke me the right way, I might purr, too. You did say you need a life, didn't you?

"I . . . I . . . aye, yi, yi," Mattie squeaked out. She'd lost it. The tenuous, fragile grip she'd had on reality was gone. It must've evaporated from lack of sleep and starvation. Her mother warned her she'd lose her marbles one day, and now she had.

Why didn't I ever listen to my mother? she asked herself. Mattie moaned as she covered her face with her hands and shook her head in utter disbelief.

Her mystery man gently took her hands from her face, then replaced them with his, softly cupping her cheeks. "It's really not that bad," he said in a soothing voice. "Think about it. Weren't you just complaining that you need more entertainment at night than an ill-mannered dog?" He raised one eyebrow and gave her a very sexy, quizzical look.

If this was just casual banter, Mattie would hate to see this guy in a boardroom. She'd never thought of herself as an easy sale, but this man was good.

Dalton's gaze never left hers as he raised one of Mattie's hands to his lips and kissed it. "Is it so hard for you to believe you are delicious in every way?" he crooned, his eyes twinkling. Then he ran his tongue over his lips in a very suggestive manner. All Mattie could do to respond was shake her head in feeble denial.

"You try hard to hide your natural sensuality, but a man, a real man, can always recognize true beauty." Dalton reached out and untied Mattie's ponytail. "Embrace it," he whispered, close enough so that Mattie could feel his breath caress her face.

He took a half step back. "Trust me?" he questioned, looking deeply into her eyes.

"Yes!" Mattie shouted with more force than she realized. Dalton gave a lusty laugh at her enthusiasm, then gently took her hand and began leading her toward the bedroom.

Oh, mama! Mattie thought. Sanity would come back, she was sure, but three years of living like a nun had its limits. Here was her chance, and every fiber of her being was screaming now! Who was she to interfere with the natural order of her body's physiology? Certainly, not her. Her mother had always told her to listen to her body, and for once in her life, by golly, she was going to listen to her mother. Even if it killed her. And since it had been three years, it just might! What a way to go, Mattie thought devilishly.

"I just want you to know," Dalton began when they'd reached the bedroom entry, "you're beautiful." He moved around her to encircle her from behind. Laying butterfly kisses on the side of her forehead, he groaned softly as he pulled her closer to him.

A deep sigh escaped Mattie's lips. Her chest heaved with desire, as his kisses traveled down her cheek and to the base of her neck. She felt his hand move slowly up to the top button of her sensible suit blouse and linger there.

"I want you, Mattie. Do you want me?"

Mattie closed her eyes as her needs screamed out a resounding, "Yes!"

Outside, Buttons barked wildly. Her eyes flew open at the distraction and she realized she'd fallen asleep at the kitchen counter.

"No!" her needs screamed again. Her dream had taken a giant nosedive, crashing and burning with no survivors left in the wreckage. A quick check of the room told here that Mr. GQ was no longer in the vicinity, Punkin had gotten at the muffins, and according to the clock on the coffee maker, she was on the verge of being seriously late for work.

Okay, maybe it won't be so bad, Mattie thought as she raced out the door and into her car. She'd make it to work on time if she pushed it, and even better, she'd have to make another batch of muffins to replace the ones Destructo-Cat had demolished during her short trip to La-La Land. The office wouldn't care if the muffins were a day late, as food, any food, was always welcomed.

As Mattie drove away, a smile spread across her face. Maybe, just maybe, she'd eat a muffin before she went to sleep. It couldn't hurt . . . right?

ooh-la-la quiche muffins

makes 12–14 muffins

1¼ cups flour

1 tablespoon baking powder

¼ teaspoon salt

1 teaspoon dried oregano

1 teaspoon dried parsley flakes

¼ teaspoon garlic powder

6 eggs, slightly beaten

½ cup salted butter, melted

¾ cup onion, finely chopped

½ cup grated Parmesan cheese

1 package (10 ounces) frozen chopped broccoli, thawed and drained

1 cup chopped mushrooms

1. Preheat oven to 375 degrees.

2. In a large bowl, mix together dry ingredients (flour through garlic powder). Form a well in the center. Set aside.

3. In a separate bowl, stir together eggs, butter, onion, cheese, broccoli, and mushrooms. Pour into dry-ingredient well and stir until just moistened.

4. Lightly grease or paper-line muffin cups. Fill each cup ¾ full. Bake 20 to 25 minutes, or until a toothpick comes out clean.

if you like ooh-la-la quiche muffins, then you'll love

Jean Luc

Let Jean Luc take you on a trip to beautiful Paris—the City of Lights. But no city light can burn as brightly as the light of love deep within this hunky Frenchman's eyes. Together, you can share an unforgettable night of romance as you climb the Eiffel Tower of desire. Oh, oui! Oui!

berry nice muffins

makes about 12 muffins

1¾ cups flour

2 teaspoons baking powder

1 cup sugar

1 egg, slightly beaten

½ cup milk

½ cup salted butter, melted

1 cup fresh raspberries

Nut Topping:

½ cup brown sugar, firmly packed

¼ cup pecans, chopped

2 tablespoons butter, melted

1. Preheat oven to 350 degrees.

2. In a large bowl, mix together dry ingredients (flour through sugar). Form a well in the center. Set aside.

3. In a separate bowl, mix together egg, milk, and butter. Pour into dry-ingredient well and stir until just moistened. Gently fold in raspberries.

4. Lightly grease or paper-line muffin cups. Fill each cup ¾ full of batter. Set aside.

5. In a small bowl, mix together topping ingredients. Sprinkle evenly over batter cups.

6. Bake 20 to 25 minutes, or until toothpick inserted in the center comes out clean. Cool 3 minutes in pan before removing.

Barry

Sweet Barry has some serious skills in the kitchen. And he doesn't ever want you to forget him, so he baked up a special signature treat—just for you. Just taste one bite of his Berry Nice Muffins, and you'll sigh with complete bliss. Wow, this man is gorgeous, thoughtful, and he can cook, too! The total package. You'll be craving Barry's Berry Nice Muffins for weeks on end.

lean and luscious mini-muffins

makes 12–14 muffins

1. Preheat oven to 375 degrees.

2. In a large bowl, mix together dry ingredients (flour through cinnamon). Form a well in the center. Set aside.

3. In a separate bowl, stir together egg whites, bananas, corn syrup, and milk. Pour into dry-ingredient well and stir until just moistened.

4 Lightly grease mini-muffin cups and fill each cup ¾ full of batter. Bake 12 to 15 minutes or until a toothpick comes out clean. Cool 5 minutes before removing from pan.

1½ cups flour

½ cup sugar

2 teaspoons baking powder

½ teaspoon salt

1 teaspoon cinnamon

2 egg whites, beaten

2 medium bananas, mashed

⅓ cup corn syrup

¼ cup milk

Work It Out

The gym felt hot and stuffy despite the blasting air-conditioning and the fact I hadn't even turned on a machine yet. As I stood on the treadmill in my oversized T-shirt and baggy sweatpants, I did what I shouldn't have—I assessed the room, comparing myself to all the toned women in their trendy sportswear who were confidently running or stair-climbing or pressing weights.

Most of them weren't even breaking a sweat. I felt very self-conscious, even though I tried to reason with myself that it was only my second visit, and the personal trainer assigned to me that first day promised me that I, too, would look that good in as little as six weeks. I should have made a deal with her. If she could morph this flabby blob of flesh into one of those hard bodies in anything less than six years, I'd give her my current weight in gold. She would be a wealthy woman, indeed.

I stared at the treadmill controls, trying to remember which buttons to push. The thing looked like the control panel of a jet airplane. I just wanted the thing under my feet to move, preferably at a slow crawl. I looked around, desperately trying to find my trainer among the sea of crowded bodies in the gym. The front desk said she was out there somewhere, but I had the feeling she was leaving me to my own devices. She probably figured I was a lost cause.

A sudden surge of determination hit me. I'll show her, I thought. Stubbornness (along with big butts) ran in my family. I'm sorry to say, both were not the best qualities I would have chosen.

After several minutes of study, I began programming the machine. I punched in all the important information: weight, age, speed, incline angle, and duration. I stopped just short of my rank and serial number. As the machine took off, I puffed along on my power walk, concentrating very hard on breathing normally, without having my tongue hang out in a pant.

I tried to find a distraction from telling myself to just quit and go home. I noticed two young women next to me, running at a good clip and effortlessly talking, nonstop. One was complaining to the other how she'd gone from a size one to a whole size three. Grrr! My mind reeled, figuring the last time I saw a size three was probably when I was three years old. I watched the two girls finish off their run and walk away, still chatting a mile a minute. I realized, at this point, that I had lost the ability to produce anything more than a grunt.

I hung onto the treadmill's side bars for support, determined not to fall on my face. Looking down at the display, I saw I still had another twenty minutes to go. I can do this, I thought, as I lifted up the bottom of my shirt and

74

used it to wipe my sweaty face. I just need a new distraction. The first thing that came to my mind was the Lean and Luscious Mini-Muffins I saw in the gym's health bar when I walked in. Of course, it'd be food—the thing that brought me to the gym in the first place. I probably should have been visualizing that little black dress I was going to fit into, but I was hungry. And I knew I couldn't eat the dress. Besides, I reasoned, the muffins are low-fat and delicious. I knew that because I had one after my first workout without any guilty feelings whatsoever. I tried closing my eyes, and I thought about muffins . . .

"Nice," I heard someone say, and my eyes flew open.

Standing to the side of the treadmill was a very muscular, reduce-me-to-liquefaction man. He wore a tank top that appeared to be painted on his body. Huge biceps bulged from the sleeve opening, and I swore he had a lot more than six in his pack, if that were humanly possible. He was pumped and toned beyond anything I'd ever seen before. I pulled my tongue back behind my teeth.

"Excuse me?" was the best I could articulate, but not without effort.

"I said, 'Nice.' It's nice to see a good-looking woman like you take care of herself," he answered. "What's your name?"

I tried to respond, but I realized I was breathing too hard to speak, even though the treadmill was barely moving. He laughed at my predicament and leaned in closer. "They call me Mav. So, are you breathing hard because of me or the workout?" he asked flirtatiously.

Mav stepped up onto the treadmill next to me and started walking, his massive body moving against mine in that narrow space. He pushed a button, and the machine sped up, slowly at first, but then picked up speed. He fell into step with the accelerating machine, and effortlessly, miraculously, so did I. A sense of elation and bliss enveloped me as the two of us ran, faster and faster, our feet barely touching the moving belt. I'd heard people talk about a runner's high. Could this be it?

"We could work out together," he told me, his voice steady and strong. "I could help you. Two hot, sweaty bodies . . . heavy breathing . . . racing hearts . . . "

Just then, salty sweat fell into my eyes, burning them. I let go of the side bars, frantically swiping at my eyes to stop the stinging. A little too late, the voice of my one-time personal trainer echoed in my head: "Always hold the bars while the machine is in motion." I lost my footing on the relentless belt, and in a very ungraceful display, I fell off the treadmill and landed on my well-padded ass in the middle of the gym floor.

It felt like all eyes in that place were on me as I sat a good three feet from the machine that had just spit me out like a bad chicken bone. All eyes, except for my Mav's. Poof. Just like that, my sexy mystery hunk had disappeared as quickly as he had shown up.

As dignified as I could manage, I lifted my sore posterior off the floor. Gathering my towel, water bottle, and what was left of my ego, I limped off to the health bar for some comfort food. I figured a mini-muffin—or twelve—would adequately ease the pain.

75

one smart cookie muffins

makes about 12 muffins

20 packaged cookies of your choice (e.g., chocolate cream sandwich, chocolate chip, peanut butter, etc.)

1¾ cups flour

½ cup sugar

1 tablespoon baking powder

½ teaspoon salt

¼ cup salted butter, melted

¾ cup milk

⅓ cup sour cream

1 egg, slightly beaten

1. Preheat oven to 375 degrees.

2. Coarsely chop cookies. Set aside.

3. In a large bowl, mix together dry ingredients (flour through salt). Form a well in the center. Set aside.

4. In a separate bowl, mix together butter, milk, sour cream, and egg. Pour into dry-ingredient well and stir until just moistened. Gently fold in chopped cookies.

5. Lightly grease or paper-line muffin cups. Fill each cup ¾ full of batter. Bake 15 to 20 minutes, or until a toothpick inserted in the center comes out clean. Cool 5 minutes before removing from the pan.

76

if you like one smart cookie muffins, then you'll love

Gabriel

Incredibly smart and business-savvy Gabriel sits behind a computer desk, and you can't help but daydream about him from the confinements of your own cubicle. His hard-core drive and determination to succeed are a huge turn-on. How ever will you be able to get this smart cookie's attention? A naughty thought crosses your mind and you glance at your watch. Looks like it's going to be a long day at the office, you smile to yourself. Even this smart cookie won't know what hit him.

wine country muffins

makes about 12 muffins

1. Preheat oven to 375 degrees.

2. In a large bowl, mix together dry ingredients (flour through salt). Form a well in the center. Set aside.

3. In a separate bowl, mix together butter, egg, cheese, wine, and chives. Pour into dry-ingredient well and stir until just moistened.

4. Lightly grease or paper-line muffin cups. Fill each cup ¾ full of batter. Bake 15 to 20 minutes, or until a toothpick inserted in the center comes out clean. Cool 5 minutes before removing from pan.

2 cups flour

1 tablespoon baking powder

1 teaspoon salt

⅓ cup salted butter, melted

1 egg, slightly beaten

1 cup grated Gruyere cheese

⅔ cup white wine

2 teaspoons chopped chives (fresh or frozen)

Wine Country

Lara watched with complete disbelief as her boss plopped another dozen or so files on top of the already teetering stack on her tiny desk. "These need to be done by tomorrow, too," he said, dispassionately, then turned without waiting for her reaction. That was a good thing, because he probably would have considered it grounds for dismissal.

She just sat there for a moment, staring at the manila mountain in front of her, wondering how her life had gone so wrong. She knew she only had herself to blame. With each turn in her life, she took the easy, safe path. She let every chance for adventure pass by, afraid to make a wrong choice. Now look where it's got me, she said to herself as she looked around her ugly, prison cell–like cubicle.

On top of being depressed, her boyfriend had been pestering her to get married and start a family. Ed came from a big family, and his dream was to have children, lots of children. More and more, Lara thought he might be happier if he married a brood mare. Once he hit twenty-five, the pressuring increased. She had heard of women with pounding biological clocks. She decided Ed had one

as large as Big Ben. But Lara was definitely not ready to settle down yet, despite his repeated attempts to get her to choose a wedding date. How could she get stuck as a housewife and mother when she felt like she hadn't lived yet, or traveled, or experienced any of those amazing or wonderful things she knew had to be out there? If she married him now, which would be the easiest, safest choice, she knew she'd be trapped forever—plain and simple.

Lara slowly opened the top file and tried to focus on the print on the first page. A sudden flash and chime on her computer diverted her attention for the twentieth time that morning. Somehow, the spam control on the office computers was down, and a continual barrage of messages—advertising everything from loan consolidation to male enhancement—kept popping up on her screen.

"Fix the computers!" she yelled at the faceless masses beyond her cubicle wall. Lara was just about to delete the message when the picture on her screen gave her pause. There, smiling at her from behind the glass was a man standing between two rows of lush, green grapevines, holding something in his hand. Lara rolled her chair in for a closer look, but the picture was too small.

Looking around to see if anyone was watching, she slid the mouse, moving the cursor over the pic-

80

ture. With a trembling hand, Lara clicked to enlarge the view. Now full-screen, she saw a man who made her quiver from the inside out. He had the look of pure manliness; handsomely virile, like the fertile fields surrounding him. His hair was the color of the dark brown earth below his feet, and his white shirt accentuated his sun-bronzed skin. In his hand wasn't a manila file, annoying Post-it notes, or a clock. Instead, he held a large crystal wine goblet, filled with deep-crimson wine. And then there was that smile. He had a smile that could make angels weep. Lara could almost feel his unadulterated passion oozing out of every pore.

She must've sat there for a good two minutes, just staring into his two-dimensional coal-colored eyes, mesmerized by the look he gave her (and she was confident he was somehow only looking at her). Finally, but not without effort, she pulled her eyes away from his face to read the text of the ad. It beckoned visitors to California's Wine Country aboard a train that meandered through the valleys of Napa and Sonoma. Her heart flip-flopped. This was exactly the kind of romantic adventure that she had always yearned to take, but was somehow afraid to. She looked back at the man with the wine glass in his hand, and her yearning only worsened.

Her moment of mental lust was shattered by her boss, who burst back into her cubicle and plunked down five more folders. "These, too," he snapped, not making eye contact or breaking his stride as he left.

A sense of deep despair, coupled by her strong, if not illogical longing for her vineyard hunk, descended on Lara like a dark cloud. She dropped her head on top of pile of files and closed her eyes . . .

A gentle rocking rhythm caused Lara to stir and lift her head. For a moment, she was confused about her surroundings, but it didn't take long for her to figure out she was traveling through a lush countryside on a fast-moving train.

Lara noticed she was alone in a luxurious train compartment. *How did I get here?* she wondered to herself. She looked back out the window and saw the bright morning sun rising over verdant rolling hills covered with rows of thick green grapevines. It was the most beautiful scene she had ever seen. She watched as the train sped perpendicularly past the long rows, and her eyes were treated with what looked like a precise and graceful march; if she looked directly out, she could see down the long rows filing by, as if they were in a big parade, but if she looked on a diagonal, it looked as if the rows were falling into sideway stacks.

The scene so entranced Lara that she didn't hear the train steward at her door until he spoke. "Next stop, Sonoma, Ma'am." She jumped, and he apologized for startling her before moving on down the aisle. A small surge of energy ran through her body. It was like she knew something exciting was about to happen, but she had no idea what it was. "Am I supposed to get off here?" she turned around to ask, but no one was there to answer.

81

The train came to a gentle stop. Not quite sure what to do, Lara got up and looked out her door, down the aisle. The train steward was out there again, motioning her to the door that led to the platform. Lara hesitated a moment, paralyzed by her usual fear of the unknown. Maybe I should just stay on the train. She felt safe on the train. Suddenly, she realized this moment summed up her entire, boring life. Yes, she was safe, but she was tired of being safe. Her whole being screamed at her to take a chance, to find her own adventure, to live. Without another second's hesitation, she strode purposely toward the exit.

Once on the platform she looked around. Now what? she thought. But she didn't have to wait long to find out as a uniformed driver approached her. Tipping his cap with his gloved hand, he said, "Welcome, Miss Lara. The car is this way." He walked off ahead of her. The old Lara would have stood there on the platform, debating if she should follow this strange man to a strange car. The new Lara almost ran to follow him. She was starting to really like the new Lara.

When they cleared the platform, Lara saw a beautiful black stretch limo with darkened windows parked against the curb. No, she thought, this can't be for me . . . She watched as the driver walked directly to the passenger door and pulled it open. "Ma'am?" He smiled at her and reached out his hand. She returned his smile with a bigger one and took his hand, climbing in with no idea of where she was going and not really caring.

She slid effortlessly into the cool leather seats. It was dark inside, and it took a moment for her eyes to adjust. Suddenly, a darkened shape across from her spoke. "Lara, my love, you are here!" said the shape with a slight Italian accent that made her name sound almost musical.

Lara drew in a quick intake of air. "Who—?" she sputtered. She squinted to make out the details in the talking shape, and she suddenly knew exactly who he was. It was her Internet macho man, only he wasn't frozen on her computer screen, and he wasn't two-dimensional. He was a living, breathing, huggable three-dimensional hunk that looked better than she ever could have imagined.

She found herself staring, gaped mouth, at the Roman statue incarnate across from her. Amused, he leaned back in his seat and gave her a smile that melted her heart and a couple of kneecaps, as well. "Come sit by Dominic, and I will show you my land." He held out his hand. She took it willingly, allowing him to pull her across to the seat next to him. There was no turning back now. She was being hurled into the best adventure she had ever had, bar none—and she loved every minute of it.

Dominic put his arm around her shoulders and leaned across her, pointing out the car window. "There, on those hills. Can you see the grapes, heavy on the vine?" Lara had trouble focusing out the window, as she was focusing on his touch. It felt so warm and strong. She forced herself to look, but she couldn't see any grapes.

82

Lara suddenly opened her eyes wide. "Yes! I do! They're the same green as the leaves," she said excitedly.

"Those are the zinfandel grapes. They are not yet ready for harvest. Probably another few weeks before they are perfect," Dominic said with tenderness in his voice, as if he were talking about his beloved children. "These make a wine that taste like raspberries and red cherries with a peppery finish. Delicious." It sounded delicious to Lara. He sounded delicious, she decided.

Dominic directed her attention out the other side of the car. "These? Pinot noir." Lara could see these dark purple grapes clearly as they hung heavy on the vine. "We will be picking these within the week," he said. "Their time has almost come."

Lara watched him as he looked out over his vineyards. She could see the love in his eyes as they passed row after row of his grapevines. She could hear the pride in his voice as he spoke about his family's history on this land. Never had she met someone with such passion about anything. Lara found his enthusiasm contagious and endearing.

The limo turned off the main road and traveled down a dirt path. "Now, my Lara, I want to show you something special." He squeezed her shoulder. He can show me anything he wants, she thought, taking this opportunity to snuggle in closer, feeling his body next to her. She had never been this bold with a man, but it felt so right and so good that she didn't care.

The limo stopped in the middle of a huge vineyard. The driver got out and opened the door. Once again, he held out his hand for Lara, and she accepted it as she stepped out onto the firmly packed earth.

As far as her eyes could see were dense bunches of blue-purple grapes tucked among the vines, thick with green leaves. Lara was struck by the sensation of the air that surrounded her. It was both warm from the sun and cool from the breeze, making her skin tingle. She breathed it in deeply, smelling the heady aroma of grape and dirt and morning mist.

Dominic walked up to Lara from behind and wrapped his arms around her waist. He nuzzled her neck, and her skin tingled again, but this time not from the air. "I brought you to one of my favorite places. These are my merlot grapes, the pride of my family's vineyard. Let me show you."

He kept one hand on her waist as he led her to a nearby vine. Brushing back the broad leaves, he revealed a thick bunch of the perfectly ripe fruit. He wrapped one of his large hands around it and gently pulled. The grapes snapped off easily.

Dominic held the bunch up so Lara could see it better. "These grapes are perfect, but not easy to grow," he said. "Planted at the wrong time or in the wrong soil, they wither and die."

He pulled off one grape and put it gently in her mouth. She bit down through the taut skin and a burst of unbelievable sweetness spread across her tongue.

It was the best thing she had ever tasted. "Oh, wow," she gushed. He smiled at her response.

Dominic placed the bunch in a small basket near the grapevine and continued. "But they are only perfect because they had a chance to grow, and in their own time. We could not rush them. If we had, the wine would not taste as sweet." He took both of Lara's hands in his and looked deeply in her eyes. "These grapes are like you, Lara. You need to find your time in the sun. Your life cannot be rushed, it cannot be forced. You must find your own fertile ground to flourish. You must take your chance to grow."

He knew. Somehow, he knew everything about her life and what she needed. "How did you know?" asked Lara as she stared deeply into his incredible eyes. Before Dominic could answer, she did the most impulsive thing she had ever done in her life. She reached up and kissed him on the lips, softly at first, then harder and more passionately. He returned her kiss, and then he drew back with a smile. "Now, my Lara, we drink the wine of these perfect grapes."

Dominic led Lara back to the limo and retrieved a picnic basket from the trunk. He put his arm around her shoulders and led her down between two rows of grapevines. Stopping mid-row, he spread out a blanket and they sat down. He pulled out a delicious assortment of crackers, fresh fruit, and his momma's special Wine Country Muffins. She tasted one, and it was simply divine.

Lastly, he brought out a bottle of his winery's merlot. He opened the bottle and poured two glasses, handing one to Lara.

"Allow me to teach you how to properly taste wine," he said, and he moved closer to her on the blanket. "First, you must look at it."

Lara held it up to the sun, marveling at the brilliance of its dark red color. "It's gorgeous," she said. She looked at Dominic's beautiful face. "Just gorgeous," she breathed, now talking about the wine and the man. He thanked her for the compliment by giving her an amazing smile.

"Next," he continued, "you must smell it. Don't be shy, just put your nose over the rim of the glass and take a deep breath. Each grape has a story to tell."

Lara, tentatively, put her nose over the edge and breathed in deeply. "Oh," she exclaimed, "I can smell cherries . . . and pears!"

He smiled at her enthusiasm. "Okay, now for the best part. We drink!" Dominic linked his arm through hers, and they held their glasses to their lips. "Take a small sip and let it roll on your tongue a bit, but don't swallow it right away."

They took a drink and Lara did as Dominic said, letting the rich wine spread over her tongue for a moment. It floated over it like silk, and the sensation was wonderful. But it was not as wonderful as the next sensation, as Dominic's mouth found hers, and together they tasted the wine in a way they never did in those tasting rooms.

84

When he pulled away, she gave him a shy grin. "Is that the way everyone tastes wine?"

"Not everyone," he replied with a small laugh. "Just those people who know how to live."

He stretched out on the blanket and pulled Lara down next to him. Together they lay in the middle of what Lara figured was heaven on earth. They drank more wine and ate more muffins. Between the warmth of the wine and the sun and Dominic's hard body pressed against hers, Lara felt like she was floating in a sea of happiness. Here she found peace and contentment. There were no boyfriends with commitment pressures, no bosses with unreasonable demands. The world was now hers for the taking. Right then and there she knew what she had to do. She had to find her own fertile ground, so she could grow and flourish. She had to take the chance before the sun passed her by.

She rose up a bit and looked at her beautiful Dominic. He slowly reached for her head, and then began pulling it toward his. "Oh, my Lara, I need—"

He stopped and looked at her with a look of desire so intense that it made her heart nearly stop. She closed her eyes, willing herself to breathe.

"What do you need, my love?" she giggled excitedly.

"I need those files by tonight at five or else!" her angry boss suddenly barked.

Lara spun around in her chair and saw her boss standing in her gray cubicle. Just like the morning mist over the vineyard, Dominic had vanished. So had the picnic blanket, the wine, and the muffins. But instead of feeling despair, she felt elation. Finally, she knew what she had to do. Her time had come.

When he pulled away, she gave him a shy grin. "Is that the way everyone tastes wine?"

Lara stood suddenly and put her hand out to stop him. "No, I need. I need fertile ground! I need my time in the sun! I need a glass of wine and a muffin! I quit!"

She grabbed her purse and ran past her very baffled boss to the parking garage. Once inside her car, she phoned a startled Ed, and in under-thirty seconds, called off their engagement. She then programmed her GPS for the train station and drove off without ever looking back.

luck of the irish muffins

makes about 12 muffins

2 cups flour

1 tablespoon baking powder

½ teaspoon salt

¾ cup sugar

1 egg, slightly beaten

⅓ cup salted butter, melted

1 cup heavy cream

½ cup sour cream

¼ cup Irish whiskey

¼ cup coffee-flavor liqueur

Topping:

2 tablespoons salted butter, melted

¼ cup sugar

1. Preheat oven to 350 degrees.

2. In a large bowl, mix together dry ingredients (flour through sugar). Form a well in the center. Set aside.

3. In a separate bowl, mix together egg, butter, heavy cream, sour cream, whiskey, and liqueur. Pour into dry-ingredient well and stir until just moistened.

4. Lightly grease or paper-line muffin cups. Fill each cup ¾ full of batter. Bake 15 to 20 minutes, or until a toothpick inserted in center comes out clean. Cool 5 minutes before removing from pan.

5. Brush muffin tops evenly with 2 tablespoons melted butter. Place ¼ cup sugar in a small bowl. Hold muffin upside down and roll tops in sugar.

if you like luck of the irish muffins, then you'll love

Sean

Let Sean make your lucky day! Who needs that gold coin or four-leaf clover when you've got this charming stud? One look at his reddish-blond hair and beautiful green eyes, and you'll be crying, "Kiss me!" whether you're Irish or not.

 # warm your heart potato cheese muffins

makes 15 muffins

1¼ cups flour

2 tablespoons sugar

2 teaspoons baking powder

1 teaspoon baking soda

1 teaspoon salt

1 cup instant potato flakes

2 eggs, beaten

1½ cups milk

¾ cup salted butter, melted

½ cup grated cheddar cheese

1. Preheat oven to 400 degrees.

2. In a large bowl, mix together dry ingredients (flour through potato flakes). Form a well in the center. Set aside.

3. In a separate bowl, stir together egg, milk, and butter. Pour into dry-ingredient well and stir until just moistened.

4. Lightly grease or paper-line muffin cups. Fill each cup ¾ full of batter. Sprinkle cheese evenly over tops. Bake 20 to 25 minutes or until cheese is browned. Cool 5 minutes before removing from pan.

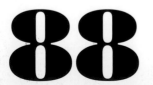

if you like warm your heart potato cheese muffins, then you'll love

Everett

Everett's your ski instructor and you can't help but stare as his strong, agile body carves the mountain effortlessly upon his skis. He laughs in the face of danger and gets an adrenaline rush from the freedom of being outdoors and moving oh-so-swiftly down the slopes. After the rigorous ski session, thaw out at the lodge and get cozy with a nice, steamy cup of hot cocoa with your teacher. Perhaps you can show him a thing or two yourself?

easy-on-the-eyes
carrot muffins makes 14 muffins

1. Preheat oven to 350 degrees.

2. In a large bowl, mix together dry ingredients (flour to chopped walnuts). Form a well in the center. Set aside.

3. In a separate bowl, stir together butter, eggs, carrots, pineapple, and vanilla extract. Pour into dry-ingredient well and stir until just moistened.

4. Lightly grease or paper-line muffin cup. Fill each cup ¾ full with batter. Bake 15 to 20 minutes or until a toothpick comes out clean. Cool 5 minutes before removing from pan.

1½ cups flour

1 tablespoon baking powder

1 teaspoon baking soda

½ teaspoon salt

1 teaspoon cinnamon

1 cup packed brown sugar

½ cup chopped walnuts

⅔ cup salted butter, melted

2 eggs, beaten

1 cup shredded carrots

1 cup crushed pineapple, drained

1 teaspoon vanilla extract

91

Easy on the Eyes

My return to Chicago was something of a rebirth for me. When I left for law school I was poor, extremely plain, a little chubby, and very shy. Worst of all, my eyesight was so bad that I was forced to wear heavy-rimmed glasses with thick Coke bottle lenses. Not exactly the best look for a young woman wanting to get dates.

Law school gave me the confidence to take charge of my life. The rigorous routine of arguing mock trials, presenting closing summations, and interacting with many other law students brought out a new me. The more confident I became, the more I wanted to change my outer appearance. I began a campaign of dieting and exercise in the gym, all topped off by running five miles, three times a week. By the time I graduated with honors, my body resembled that of a veteran runner. I had trim, muscular legs, a tight, hard stomach, and best of all, the loss of all the weight accentuated my natural assets in all the right places. The one thing, however, that I couldn't fix through diet and exercise was my very poor eye sight. I still had to wear eyeglasses. Even though I could now afford designer frames and lenses, without them I was nearly legally blind.

I returned to Chicago after being offered a great job at a well-known, but not famous, law firm. My first task was to find a place that I could afford in a nice part of town. After several weeks of looking at dumps, I found the perfect one-bedroom apartment on the lake. My trusty golden retriever puppy and running partner, Sam, and I moved in as soon as we could.

I quickly resumed my routine of running and exercise. I especially enjoyed running with Sam along the shoreline park of Lake Michigan. Sam enjoyed the runs as much as I did, but unfortunately sometimes he'd get carried away, splashing in the water or chasing squirrels. Oh, he could be a handful!

On one cold and crisp October morning, Sam and I were running our usual route along the shoreline when Sam spotted a particularly sinister-looking squirrel peering from behind a tree. Because I was in the zone while running, it took a few seconds for me to realize that he had yanked me off balance and into the path of a man walking in my direction. With a loud thud, we both fell to the ground, with me landing on top of him. I lost my grip on Sam's leash, and he took off immediately. In a panic, I realized that my glasses

92

had flown off, and the whole world became an instant fuzzy blur.

"I'm so sorry I ran into you, miss," the stranger said in a deep, soothing voice, "I didn't see you."

"No, no, it was my fault. My dog pulled me off balance and I hit you," I said frantically feeling the ground around me. "Do you see my glasses anywhere? Without them I'm nearly blind, and I need to find Sam."

The deep, inviting voice said, "I'm sorry, miss, but it looks like there's a problem. I think we must have landed on your glasses when we fell. They look useless to me. Let me help you up, and we'll find a bench to sit on for a minute. Then I'll find your dog for you. What's his name? Sam?"

"Yes, Sam. I can't thank you enough. He's a golden retriever puppy with a green leash and collar," I replied. Even though my eyesight was blurry, I could tell this man had a strong, muscular body that someday (hopefully that day) I would see.

After sitting on the bench for what seemed to be an eternity, I finally heard my unseen stranger talking to Sam. I squinted, but I couldn't see a thing. I was startled and let out a short scream when I felt the stranger's hand touch my shoulder from behind and, two seconds after, Sam jumping all over me. I needed my glasses fixed, and soon.

"Sorry. Didn't mean to scare you," he apologized. "I found Sam over by that large oak tree. He was terrorizing a squirrel he had chased up it. May I have a seat next to you?"

"Please do. I'm afraid I'm at your mercy without my glasses," I smiled pathetically. My mother would have had a conniption if she knew I was divulging so much information to a perfect stranger, but I didn't care. All I knew was that I wanted to get to know my hero a lot better. Sliding to the side, I felt him sit next to me. I could feel the warmth of his body radiating onto mine. I finally felt safe.

"I'm Sally," I said, offering out my hand.

Taking my small hand in his large and inviting hand, he said, "And I'm Rick. So how long have you had to wear glasses?"

"All my life. It's been my Achilles' heel, so to speak," I said shyly.

"Well, Sally, I think I can help you with that," said Rick matter-of-factly. "If you'll trust me just a little bit longer, I think we can solve your problem. Just wait."

At that point, Rick stood up, and I could hear him hail a cab. He took me gently by the hand and carefully helped Sam and me in before squeezing himself

93

in beside us. He rattled off an address to the driver so quickly that I was unable to hear where we were going. I started to get butterflies in my stomach not knowing what was going to happen next. I just kept hoping Sam would protect me by turning into a snarling, vicious guard dog if circumstances warranted. Once, of course, he was finished slobbering all over Rick, his new best friend.

To heck with the world! I thought. I'd seen the world before.

After a short drive, we arrived at our destination. All I could see was the shiny reflection of steel and glass. I heard Rick tell the cabbie to keep the change, and then he led Sam and me to the entrance.

"This is it, Sally," Rick said with a twinge of excitement in his voice. Unlocking the door, he escorted us to an elevator. "My place is on the seventh floor."

Arriving on the seventh floor, he directed us to another door. With a loud click, the door was unlocked and Rick exclaimed, "Welcome to Johnson Optometry. I'm your host, Dr. Johnson."

At first I was confused, but once Rick explained that he was an optometrist, it suddenly made sense why he was so interested in my eyes. Again, I felt so safe and protected with him.

"You know, Sally, a beautiful woman like you shouldn't be stuck wearing glasses. I can help you with laser eye surgery and fix your eyes permanently, if you will let me," the good doctor said. Helpful, kind, complimentary . . . was there no end to this guy's good qualities?

I graciously accepted his offer. Had it not been for Dr. Johnson, I would have lost my puppy in the park and would probably still be wandering, searching in vain for my broken glasses. "I'm all yours, Doctor," I said, opening my arms and smiling flirtatiously.

Rick guided me toward the chair and lifted me up. Good voice and strong muscles. My list of non-visual attributes continued to grow. He made sure I was comfortable and then explained that the first step was to get the correct measurements of my eyes for the laser machine. As in the park, I could again feel the heat from Rick's body when his lean thigh pressed against mine as he moved in for a closer examination. I just hoped he couldn't feel my heart pounding. He moved in even closer, and his face was mere inches from mine. Oh, how I wished I could focus! It was then that I discovered his next attribute: he wore expensive cologne that smelled really, really good.

He shined a bright light into each of my eyes. "Your eyes are so beautiful, like the rest of you," he murmured. With that, my insides turned to mush.

Okay, I thought, even if he looks like Frankenstein, I don't think I'll care.

He suddenly stepped away, and I could hear him moving some equipment around. He returned quickly, and again placed his big, strong hand on my shoulder. "In just a few moments you will be able to see the world clearly." *To heck with the world!* I thought. I'd seen the world before. What did he look like? The suspense was driving me crazy.

In a matter of moments, the surgery was completed. Dr. Johnson put some eye drops in my eyes and told me to keep them shut for a few minutes. "The next time you open your eyes, you won't believe the difference."

I couldn't wait to open my eyes and when Dr. Johnson finally spoke, he said, "Take a look, Sally."

I slowly opened my eyes, blinked a few times, and instantly my world became crystal clear. The first thing—the only thing—I saw standing before me was the most handsome man imaginable. Tall, muscular, incredible smile, beautiful eyes, immaculate white lab coat . . . he had it all. I kept blinking, thinking it might just be an optical illusion, a side effect from the procedure. But the more I looked, the better he began to look.

"Now," he said rather coyly, "I have a special prescription for you." He held out the oddest thing. "It's my special carrot muffin. I make them myself and give them to all my patients. They'll help keep your vision clear."

I took a bite. It was heavenly. Okay, I ticked off in my head, good voice, strong, unbelievably cute, smells good—and he bakes! I silently thanked Sam for flunking obedience school.

"Seriously, how can I repay you?" I asked.

He smiled and winked. "I'm sure we can think of something."

He leaned in and gave me a soft, gentle kiss. And I knew we'd be seeing a lot more of each other.

tart and tasty muffins

makes about 12 muffins

2½ cups flour

½ cup sugar

1 tablespoon baking powder

½ teaspoon salt

1 egg, slightly beaten

1 cup buttermilk

⅓ cup butter, melted

1 teaspoon vanilla extract

¼ cup lime juice

2 tablespoons lime zest

Topping:

2 tablespoons salted butter, melted

¼ cup sugar

1. Preheat oven to 350 degrees.

2. In a large bowl, mix together dry ingredients (flour to salt). Form a well in the center. Set aside.

3. In a separate bowl, mix together egg, buttermilk, butter, vanilla extract, lime juice, and lime zest. Pour into dry-ingredient well and stir until just moistened.

4. Lightly grease or paper-line muffin cups. Fill each cup ¾ full of batter. Bake 15 to 20 minutes, or until toothpick inserted in center comes out clean. Cool 5 minutes before removing from pan.

5. Brush muffin tops evenly with 2 tablespoons melted butter. Place ¼ cup sugar into a small bowl. Hold muffin upside down and roll tops in sugar to coat.

if you like tart and tasty muffins, then you'll love

Dixon

Delicious Dixon lives in the hot and sultry Florida Keys. His two greatest passions are women and . . . limes. Yes, limes! Dixon likes to think that he'll one day find that special woman who is both tart and sweet at the same time. Do you think you have what it takes to be this rugged man's main squeeze?

give me s'more muffins

makes about 12 muffins

1. Preheat oven to 375 degrees.

2. In a large bowl, mix together dry ingredients (cracker crumbs through baking powder). Form a well in the center. Set aside.

3. In a separate bowl, mix together milk, egg, and honey. Fold in chocolate chips and 1 cup of marshmallows. Pour into dry-ingredient well and stir until just moistened.

4. Lightly grease or paper-line muffin cups. Fill each cup ¾ full. Sprinkle remaining ¼ cup marshmallows evenly over batter.

5. Bake 15 to 20 minutes or until a toothpick comes out clean. Cool 5 minutes before removing from pan.

2½ cups graham cracker crumbs (about 30 squares)

¼ cup sugar

2 teaspoons baking powder

1 cup milk

1 egg, slightly beaten

2 tablespoons honey

¾ cup milk chocolate chips

1¼ cups miniature marshmallows, divided

99

Give Me S'More, Please

Amber hated camping. Yet, somehow, her boyfriend, Keith, talked her into it. So there she sat, three hours from nowhere, covered in mosquito bites and nursing a huge blister from the ten-mile nature hike. On top of that, she learned there were no shower facilities anywhere near the campsite. She was dirty, itchy, and having a really bad hair day.

Now Keith wanted to make s'mores over a hot, smoky fire. Amber told him that she had brought a batch of s'more muffins she made in her nice, clean, air-conditioned kitchen instead. But no, that would take away from the authentic camping experience, Keith had argued. So off he went to gather more wood to make a campfire. *Maybe it can be large enough to become a signal fire so I can be rescued from nature hell*, Amber thought to herself.

Minutes dragged to an hour, and she was becoming desperately bored communing with nature. Staring at a tree didn't do much for her. Amber was also getting colder, as the sinking sun cast longer shadows. She began to get fidgety and looked at the small pile of wood with the pack of matches next to it. How hard could starting a fire be? She piled up the logs, added some kindling, and struck a match. The flames came to life and immediately began to flare beautifully. "Ha! I can be as outdoorsy as the next," she gloated to absolutely no one.

Just then Amber heard footsteps coming toward her direction. Keith was back, finally. The show-off in her made her throw all the kindling on, just to prove to him that she wasn't some helpless camping girly girl. But the last of the kindling was damp, causing a plume of thick smoke to envelop her head. She couldn't breathe, and the world went dark.

". . . Are you okay?" A deep sultry voice floated to her through the haze.

Amber tried desperately to clear her head, but everything was still fuzzy. When she struggled to focus, all she could see were two large, sensitive blue eyes.

"Are you an . . . angel?" she asked weakly.

"No," he chuckled softly. "I'm Blade."

Amber felt his powerful hands help her up to her feet. He still towered over her, looking as massive as a giant redwood. She didn't mean to stare, but she had to. Blade's tanned face was ruggedly handsome, and Amber never knew plaid flannel could make her heart race so much.

"Here, sit down for a moment." Amber felt Blade's strong hand now in the small of her back as he guided her to a tree stump surrounded by soft moss and wildflowers.

100

Two wild rabbits scampered away as he gently helped her down. He looked even bigger as he leaned over her.

"I guess camping doesn't really agree with me," Amber muttered, sheepishly.

"I don't know about that," he said giving her an appreciative look over. "You look pretty amazing to me."

"No, I don't—" she began to protest, but then stopped as she looked down. Gone were her dirty jeans and muddy boots. Instead, Amber wore a snow-white dress made of the softest silk that billowed gently in the breeze. Delicate sandals hugged her perfectly manicured feet. She touched her hair and felt wild daisies tucked in her long, cascading, glistening locks. She loosened one of the flowers, and Blade stepped closer.

"Here, let me fix that," he said as he ever so gently reached for the flower. His touch took Amber's breath away, and this time it was definitely not from smoke inhalation. She grabbed Blade's arm to steady herself—his big, bronzed, tree trunk of an arm—and held on just a little longer than necessary.

"Could I get you something?" He reached out and cupped her face with his hands. "Some water? Perhaps a little something to eat?" He moved closer, pressing his body to hers.

As Amber stared up into those sultry, clear eyes, she realized that she already had what she wanted. But she was having trouble thinking clearly.

"Maybe s'mores?" she breathed. "We could start a nice little fire."

Blade gave her a sultry smile. "I believe we already have. Besides, I think I know what you really want." He picked up her backpack. "May I?" he asked, and she nodded. Slowly, he reached inside and pulled out the perfect muffin, loaded with chocolate, marshmallows, and graham crackers. Kneeling down beside her, he held the muffin out, and Amber took a bite. It was pure heaven—sweet, creamy, moist.

Once he saw she was satisfied, Blade leaned in, his face gently brushing hers. She breathed in his scent of pine needles, freshly hewn wood, and chocolate.

"Want s'more?" he whispered huskily in her ear.

"Yes! Oh, yes!" Amber could hardly control her anticipation.

Suddenly, the world spun again. Sputtering and gasping, she found herself flat on her back next to the fire, covered in sooty smoke residue. Keith was standing over her.

No! Oh, no! Blade was gone. Her dress was gone. The wild rabbits were gone.

"Make up your mind. Are you all right or not?" Keith asked, seeming somewhat annoyed.

"Yeah, I'm fine," Amber groaned as she struggled to her feet. Where there had once been flowers, she now had twigs and leaves irretrievably entangled in her hair.

"Do you still want to make s'mores?" he asked.

"No! The fire's out. Just give me a muffin," Amber disappointedly sighed. Keith shrugged and handed one over to her. As she took a bite a smile crept across her face. It wasn't the same but it would have to do.

101

pear me up muffin

makes 12–15 muffins

3 tablespoons butter, melted

²/₃ cup brown sugar

¼ cup almonds, finely chopped

2 cups flour

1 tablespoon baking powder

½ teaspoon salt

2 teaspoons cinnamon

1 egg, slightly beaten

1 cup milk

¼ cup salted butter, melted

1 cup peeled and diced
   fresh pear

1. Preheat oven to 350 degrees.

2. In a small bowl, stir together 3 tablespoons butter, brown sugar, and almonds. Evenly spoon mixture into lightly greased muffin cups. Set aside.

3. In a large bowl, mix together dry ingredients (flour through cinnamon). Form a well in the center. Set aside.

4. Pour into dry-ingredient well and stir until just moistened. In a separate bowl, mix together egg, milk, and butter. Gently fold in pears.

5. Fill each muffin cup ¾ full of batter. Bake 15 to 20 minutes, or until a toothpick comes out clean. Cool 3 minutes. Invert pan and serve muffins upside down.

if you like pear me up muffins, then you'll love

Jordan

Jordan runs a wildly popular dating service. He vows to "pear" you up with the man of your dreams! On your dreamy dates you'll enjoy hot, steamy dinners and fresh, cool desserts of strawberries, raspberries, and peaches. But, you seem to long for that one dessert that only Jordan can bring. Will this hunky man be a match made entirely for you?

after-dinner mint muffins makes 15–18 muffins

½ cup salted butter

1 cup semisweet chocolate chips

2 cups flour

1 tablespoon baking powder

1 teaspoon salt

½ cup sugar

½ cup milk

1 egg, slightly beaten

⅔ cup sour cream

1 cup chocolate-covered thin mints, coarsely chopped

1. Preheat oven to 350 degrees.

2. In a small microwave-safe bowl, combine butter and chocolate chips. Microwave on high for 30 seconds, then stir. Repeat until chocolate is melted and mixture is smooth. (If you do not have a microwave, melt butter and chocolate in a small saucepan over low heat, stirring constantly until chocolate is melted and mixture is smooth.) Set aside to cool slightly.

3. In a large bowl, mix together dry ingredients (flour through sugar). Form a well in the center. Set aside.

4. In a separate bowl, mix together milk, egg, and sour cream. Stir in chocolate mixture until smooth. Pour into dry-ingredient well and stir until just moistened.

5. Lightly grease or paper-line muffin cups. Fill each cup ⅔ full of batter. Place about 1 tablespoon of the chopped mints in the center of each batter cup, pressing down lightly. Bake 15 to 20 minutes, or until toothpick comes out clean. (There might be melted chocolate on the toothpick. Check for the batter to be done.)

104

if you like after-dinner mint muffins, then you'll love

Kyle

You've just finished a late dinner and dessert, and you definitely don't think you can eat anything else. That's when Kyle offers you an after-dinner mint. His alluring looks and breezy chuckle leave you feeling cool and tingly all over. He's impossible to resist, and finally you give in to temptation. The mint melts in your mouth and immediately you yearn for more . . .

tropical lei muffins

makes about 18 muffins

1. Preheat oven to 425 degrees.

2. In a large bowl, mix together dry ingredients (flour through brown sugar). Form a well in the center. Set aside.

3. In a separate bowl, mix together egg, sour cream, pineapple with the juice, coconut, and butter. Pour into dry-ingredient well and stir until just moistened.

4. Lightly grease or paper-line muffin cups. Fill each cup ¾ full of batter. Bake 15 to 20 minutes or until a toothpick comes out clean. Cool 5 minutes before removing from pan.

2 cups flour

2 teaspoons baking powder

½ teaspoon baking soda

1 package (3.4 ounces) instant vanilla pudding mix

½ cup chopped macadamia nuts

¾ cup brown sugar

1 egg, beaten

1 cup sour cream

1 can (8 ounces) crushed pineapple, reserving juice

½ cup flaked coconut

½ cup salted butter, melted

A Paradise Retreat

The morning had gotten off to a rough start. Everyone overslept, causing Kendra's oldest kids to make a mad dash for the school bus, which made the dog bark in the midst of the excitement, which then made the baby cry and drop her cup of juice all over the floor. Kendra's mother called at the height of the insanity, and the last thing she needed was to hear the tone in her mother's voice. "Sounds like Bedlam, again," her mother said, disapprovingly. "I'll call back later."

Kendra's husband rushed past her and out the door, barely brushing a kiss across her cheek. When he called back that he wouldn't be home for dinner, she slumped against the counter covered in dirty dishes. But then she saw it. There, in the midst of all the clutter, was her solace: the last pineapple macadamia nut muffin. As she took the first bite of the tender, moist, and fluffy treat she closed her eyes and drifted away . . .

Kendra was on a deserted beach, listening to the lulling melody of the waves lapping rhythmically against the shore. The air, warm and heady with the scent of white orchids and Kahili ginger blossoms, wafted sensually around her, demanding that she breathe heavily to draw it all in.

She dug her toes lazily into the powdery, white sand as the sun caressed her body like a masseuse with a thousand warm, solid hands. Just when she thought it couldn't get any better, she heard him.

"Your skin is so beautiful, but so fair," came the gentle voice from behind her. Kendra turned and saw a man—no, an ancient tribal god—standing over her, shading her with his massive muscular frame. The wind ruffled his ebony hair and his skin glistened in the sun like a melted milk chocolate Dove bar. He wore nothing but a lei and sarong that flapped up slightly in the breeze, revealing more of his lean thigh.

He knelt next to her and gave her a dazzlingly white smile, as if his teeth were made of pearl. "I am Kaunu." He picked up her bottle of sunscreen. ". . . May I?"

He did not wait for her to answer. His soft but firm fingers deftly spread the sun-warmed lotion up and down Kendra's back, making her shiver all over despite the incredible heat.

"Kaunu?" she asked. Her voice sounded strained. "That's an exotic name."

"It means 'passion,'" he breathed into her ear.

Yes, I bet it does, Kendra thought as her heart began to pound rapidly.

108

When he finished massaging the lotion all over her skin, Kaunu slowly pulled Kendra to her feet. Taking the lei from his own neck, he placed it tenderly over her head. He was now so close she could take in the aroma of fresh pineapples and coconuts from his deeply tanned skin. They breathed in unison. "Come with me. Let me show you the beauty of my island," he murmured.

He took Kendra's hand and together they walked along the shore. They didn't speak much, so as not to spoil the splendor that surrounded them. She looked around and tried to take it all in, but it was almost too overwhelming. To the right was the never-ending ocean with its whitecaps and pounding surf that sprayed a fine mist, keeping them cool and invigorated. She loved the way the surf rolled up and covered her feet, then pulled away. Each time, it felt like the ocean was gently pulling her in, tantalizing her with the possibilities of what other wonders might be hiding beneath its surface.

Little white crabs scuttled in the hard-packed sand around their feet, looking very busy, but with what, she couldn't tell. Seagulls soared gracefully over the water, diving and swooping effortlessly. Several dolphins could be seen arcing through the surface of the water in an effortless ballet. For a moment, she wished she could swim out and join them, to feel the freedom of having an entire ocean as her playground.

When Kendra looked to the left, she could see the lush, green vegetation that skirted the beach, so dense that the ground completely disappeared. There were palm trees and coconut trees, along with hundreds of plants she couldn't identify, all packed in tightly together. Many of them boasted an array of the most incredible flowers she had ever seen. Their petals were large and supple, and she couldn't imagine how lucky the hummingbirds must feel.

"It's so beautiful here," she whispered, not knowing what other words to say.

"You only add to its beauty," Kaunu replied. "Like a perfect flower." He walked over to one of the nearby plants and carefully snapped off an incredibly vibrant purple orchid. Reaching up, he gently tucked it behind her ear and brushed his hand delicately over her cheek. Again, he gave her that smile that softened her knees.

"Come," he said, pulling her gently up the beach. They continued walking and he led her to a place where the vegetation gave way to an outcrop of large rocks. Tucked behind a small opening was a small cave, lit from above from a crevasse where the rocks didn't quite meet. There, on the sandy ground, was a green thatched mat. Spread out on it was an incredible feast of tropical delicacies. "How did—?" Kendra began.

tropical lei muffins

Kaunu gently placed his index finger to her lips to silence her. "Island magic. Always trust, never question." The two sat on the mat and Kaunu started taking fresh fruit and placing it into Kendra's mouth. One by one, he placed a morsel from each dish in her mouth, and after each swallow, she couldn't fathom that anything could taste better. The spread was unbelievable: slow-roasted Kalua pork, macadamia nuts, fresh pineapple and mangoes, coconut-crusted shrimp, traditional poi, laulau, banana guava pie, and frosty mai tais garnished with beautiful orchids to wash it all down. Maybe it was the ambiance, more than likely it was the company, but Kendra knew this was the best meal she had ever had.

After several hours of delicious food and light conversation, they strolled back out on the beach at a very leisurely pace, rather sated from their tropical lunch. There was not another soul in sight, as it had been that way since she met him. It was as if they were the only two people on the island, as if it were theirs for the taking. They walked along in content silence, not needing to talk to understand each other. *More island magic,* she thought.

Kendra and Kaunu walked along the sand, hand in hand, until the sun began to set. The tide started coming in, making the waves almost explode against the rocky shore. Kaunu turned toward the sea and led Kendra toward a small protrusion of volcanic rock at the edge of the surf. He climbed effortlessly to the top and then reached down to help her up.

She was not so comfortable once off the sand. Her feet were unsteady, and as the next wave crashed, it nearly knocked her down. Instinctively, Kendra reached for him to keep her balance. Kaunu caught her in his strong arms and pulled her to him, holding her tightly. His strong muscles, rock hard from years of climbing rocks like these, steadied her as the next wave washed over their feet. "I won't let the sea take you," he said, looking deeply at her. "You're mine." Their eyes met and held. Then, as if controlled by a power stronger than the wind and the sun and the sea—the phone rang.

Nooo! Kendra thought and immediately broke out of her trance to go answer it. "Aloha?"

"Aloha?" her mother asked again with that same motherly tone. "What's going on over there now?"

Kendra's heart sank in despair as Kaunu and her private paradise dissolved into her reality of dirty dishes and sticky floors.

"Nothing, Mom," she sighed, looking around the room. Then it dawned on her what she must do. "I'm just getting ready to make some more muffins. Lots and lots of muffins."

110

sweet as pumpkin pie muffins

makes 15–18 muffins

1½ cups flour

1 cup sugar

1 teaspoon baking powder

½ teaspoon baking soda

¼ teaspoon ground cloves

1 teaspoon ground cinnamon

¼ teaspoon ground nutmeg

2 eggs, slightly beaten

¼ cup salted butter, melted

¼ cup milk

¾ cup canned pumpkin

¾ cup semisweet chocolate chips

1. Preheat oven to 400 degrees.

2. In a large bowl, mix together dry ingredients (flour through nutmeg). Form a well in the center. Set aside.

3. In a separate bowl, stir together eggs, butter, milk, and pumpkin. Fold in chocolate chips. Pour into dry-ingredient well and stir until just moistened.

4. Lightly grease or paper-line muffin cups. Fill each cup ¾ full. Bake 20 to 25 minutes, or until toothpick comes out clean.

112

if you like sweet as pumpkin pie muffins, then you'll love

Bailey

The cool autumn air ruffles Bailey's sandy hair as he leads you through a patch of pumpkins ready for harvest. He's spending this beautiful afternoon with you instead of going to the game with his friends. What a sweetie! You find the perfect one; it's ripe for the picking, just like Bailey's love for you. He lifts the huge pumpkin effortlessly to his broad shoulder, his muscles bulging and rippling. As he carries it back, you follow, enjoying the spectacular view from behind.

southern charm pecan muffins

makes 15–18 muffins

1. Preheat oven to 350 degrees.

2. In a large bowl, mix together dry ingredients (flour through pecans). Form a well in the center. Set aside.

3. In a separate bowl, mix together butter and eggs. Pour into dry-ingredient well and stir until just moistened.

4. Lightly grease or paper-line muffin cups. Fill each cup ¾ full of batter. Bake for 20 to 25 minutes, or until a toothpick comes out clean.

1 cup flour

2 cups packed brown sugar

1 teaspoon baking soda

2 cup chopped pecans

1⅓ cups salted butter, melted

3 eggs, slightly beaten

115

Southern Charmed

Rhonda was the first to admit she had a problem: she was a carboholic. It had been the bane of her existence since childhood, ever since her mother insisted no meal was complete without at least two starchy side dishes, bread and butter, and a dessert.

By the time she hit adulthood, she realized she had to do something about her addiction. She tried going cold turkey, but that usually lasted less than a day. She tried every diet known to man, hoping that a change in her overall eating would cure her dependency. All she ended up with were a stack of miracle books and lost hours of her life spent at support group meetings, cheering on someone who shed half of a pound that week. Meanwhile, her weight hardly budged.

Rhonda walked into the lunchroom at work one Monday and plopped down next to her friend, Marlene. Dramatically, she let her head fall onto the tabletop with a soft thud.

"I am a humongous pig," she moaned. "I ate a whole box of Twinkies last night."

"Another bad date on Saturday?" asked Marlene, smiling sympathetically. She'd known her friend long enough to equate a lousy first date with the annihilation of a baked good. And this was the natural progression of her rants. It went from her problems with food to her problems with men.

"Right up there with the worst," she said as she rolled back into an upright position. "When he came to pick me up, he stayed in his car, just beeping his horn, like he was calling a dog or something. Then we went to this crappy little bar where he played pool with his friends most of the night. When dinner came, he pretended he didn't have enough money, so I ended up paying for my meal and part of his. What a loser he was. What a loser I am."

Marlene rubbed her back, knowing she was just about to give her friend yet another pep talk about food and men. "You're not a loser. You're a good person, with a particularly discriminating palate for refined wheat products and really bad luck with blind dates."

Rhonda halfway lifted her head and shot her a look of disdain. "Why can't I find a nice guy, a guy with manners and charm and grace?" she said.

"Because guys like that only live in romance novels," sighed Marlene.

"But even if I ever found one, he'd be gone as soon as he saw the real me scarf down an entire pecan pie," Rhonda said. "It's just not ladylike."

116

"Stop it. I hate when you put yourself down like that," Marlene said, touching her friend's elbow. What if you tried something like, oh, I dunno . . . hypnotherapy or whatnot?"

"Yeah, I've heard about that," said Rhonda, thinking it over. "They say it can do amazing things. You go to sleep, they fill your head with negative thoughts about stuff—like eating or smoking—and then you supposedly wake up completely cured."

Wake up completely cured. That's exactly what Rhonda had dreamed and wished for all her life. "You know what? I think I'm going to give it a try!" she said resolutely as she popped the last stale muffin left over from that morning's meeting in her mouth.

Rhonda spent the next few days researching local hypnotherapists. She finally settled on a Dr. Janet Meyers, who was both a psychiatrist and certified practitioner of hypnosis. She figured if she somehow went whacko from the session, her bases would be covered for medical treatment. She made an appointment for the following day.

When Rhonda arrived at the doctor's office, she was escorted into an elegant room with cherry wood furniture and soft leather couches. The décor looked like something from an old Southern plantation, and she felt like Scarlett O'Hara standing in the middle of Tara. *That's when men were chivalrous and kind,* she thought to herself as she scanned the doctor's credentials that were framed on the wall. She grinned as another thought crossed her mind. *And I wish I could have lived back then, especially with those hoop skirts. No one could tell how big your butt was.*

Within moments, Dr. Meyers entered. She was a soft-spoken woman, and after a few pleasantries, she got right down to business.

"So, Rhonda, what brings you here today?" she asked, pen at the ready on her clipboard.

Rhonda took a deep breath and said, "I'm not crazy. I just can't stop eating anything high in carbohydrates. Can you fix me?"

Dr. Meyers gave Rhonda the same sympathetic smile her friend was used to giving her. "No," she began, "but you can fix yourself. If you're ready, I'm going to put you under hypnosis and take you back to where this problem began. Then, while you're there, you will have the power to nip it in the bud, so to speak. When I bring you back, you'll continue to have this control over the situation. Ready to give it a try?"

Go back to where the problem began? She imagined it would be her early childhood. She was nervous but excited at the same time. "I'm ready."

Dr. Meyers had Rhonda lie back on one of the squishy couches and close her eyes. "I'm going to start counting back," said Dr. Meyers in her soft voice. "As

117

I do, you will get more and more rested. By the time I get to zero, I want you to take yourself back to where you first believe your problem began. Here we go . . . "

Rhonda took a deep breath and listened as the doctor started from thirty and counted down. By the time she got to twenty, Rhonda could feel her body sink deeper into the couch. At ten, Rhonda was starting to feel almost light-headed. The closer Dr. Meyers got to zero, the stranger Rhonda felt.

". . . three, two, one . . . " Rhonda felt like she was swimming through fog. ". . . zero."

Rhonda blinked her eyes open and looked around. She expected to see her mother's small kitchen, complete with a pie cooling on the counter. Instead, she saw the same furniture and the same cherry wood from the doctor's office. "It didn't work," she muttered, disappointedly.

Rhonda swung her legs over the edge of the couch and heard a strange rustling sound. She looked down, almost as in slow motion, to see a huge ruffled skirt where her pant legs should have been. She leapt off the couch and looked at herself. Somehow, she was now wearing a full-on antebellum dress with what looked like dozens of yards of fabric. She ran to the large mirror on the wall. The reflection showed her face and arms and hands, but the rest was pure Scarlett, hoop skirt and all.

Rhonda looked around. "Uh, Dr. Meyers?" she called out timidly. There was no answer. ". . . Momma?" Nothing.

She was on the verge of a major panic attack when she heard footsteps outside the door. "Dr. Meyers!" she said, totally relieved.

The door opened, but it definitely was not her doctor or her momma. In walked the most incredible man Rhonda had ever seen, or even imagined. He had the face that was perfection personified—square jaw, high cheekbones, wide-set hazel eyes, hair the color of golden honey. It took her a moment to look past his face to notice the rest of him. He had to be well over six feet and very well built under his topcoat with its wide shoulders cut perfectly to show off the narrowness of his high-waist trousers.

Rhonda could only stare as he carried a tray with a clear glass pitcher filled with lemonade and two glasses and set it down on the table next to her. Next to that was a plate covered with a linen napkin.

"Have a nice nap, Sugar?" he asked, in his smooth-as-honey Southern drawl.

Rhonda gaped blankly at him. "Huh?" was the best she could do.

"I said, 'Did you have a nice nap?'" He smiled warmly at her, and she couldn't help but return it to him, whoever he was.

"You look a little flushed. Are you warm, Lamb?" he asked, gently placing the back of his hand to her forehead. She nodded dumbly. She was actually heating up, but she believed it wasn't from the air temperature.

118

Her Southern charmer held out his arm. "You know, it's a glorious day today. I believe you will feel a mite better if we took some lemonade out on the veranda."

Rhonda, now completely mystified, decided to go along with the romance novel that was playing out in front of her. She took his arm and held on with both hands, leaning heavily on him. He felt very good—big, strong, solid. He picked up the tray and led her to the door. Stopping to open it, he bowed slightly as he allowed her to go first. "Wow! A real gentleman . . ." were her first words, and she was shocked to hear that she had a soft drawl, as well.

"Well, I most certainly hope so," he said. "My mama would be sorely disappointed if I had turned out any other way. But you can also call me Michael." He gave her a wink as she took his arm again.

It was gorgeous outside. The veranda wrapped around the length of the house, overlooking a vast green yard dotted with large magnolia trees. Daylight hours were drawing to a close, and the shadows from the setting sun lay softly over the land, making it look like a beautiful watercolor painting.

Michael walked her toward a small table and a couple of chairs. As he placed the tray on the table, Rhonda started to sit down, but he grabbed her hand. Looking around to see if anyone was near, he quickly spirited her down the veranda steps and off across the grass to the far side of the house. Rhonda looked at him, puzzled, but he just gave her a smile that didn't look quite as proper as the one he gave her in the house. A little bolt of electricity shot through her body as she followed this mystery Southern charmer to wherever he wanted to take her.

When they reached a corner where the house cut in a bit, he pushed her gently but firmly against the wall. After another quick scan for possible prying eyes, Michael pressed his body against hers and gave her a long, passionate kiss. Rhonda, at first shocked, decided not to protest, and kissed him back. After a long minute, he pulled away. She found herself having trouble breathing, partly from the corset she wore under her dress, partly because her Southern gentleman wasn't a complete gentleman.

"I've been waiting all day for this," he whispered in her ear. "I hope you don't find me too scandalous."

She could only shake her head. He wrapped his arms around her and she returned his embrace, at which time she discovered that behind the thick, woolen waistcoat lurked the body of a massive hunk. She wondered how scandalous he'd find her if she tore that coat off his body and ran her hands over his naked chest? Just the thought made her breathing labored again.

Michael thoughtfully loosened his hold a bit, giving her a little more room to draw in a breath. He pulled back and his look burned a hole in her soul. "Would though I could, I'd get you out of that corset," he said with a look that was anything but mannered.

119

That was all she needed to hear, and her heart hammered in her heaving chest. She started feeling lightheaded again. "Oh, my stars," she said. She believed she was about to swoon, and she grabbed hold of him. Without hesitation, he picked her up like she was a doll and carried her back to the veranda. Suddenly, her proper gentleman had returned.

Rhonda couldn't quite recall what had just happened, but there was one thing she knew for sure. She was cured.

"Let's get you some lemonade," he said. Then, drawing in close, he whispered, "Until tomorrow, my love."

How long can I stay hypnotized? Rhonda thought. *One more day? Please?*

Michael gently placed her in a chair and poured her a cool glass of lemonade. It tasted amazing, obviously not made from a packet of dry powder. He then reached over and picked up the plate covered with the linen napkin.

"Mrs. Simons sent these over," he said, removing the napkin to reveal a half dozen perfect pecan muffins. "She noticed how much you enjoyed them. I do believe you ate all the ones at her last barbeque, if I'm not mistaken," he said with a playful grin. "Maybe you can save me one this time, Sugar. All right?"

They looked incredible, and she had to have one. She shot her hand out, and then stopped short. Suddenly, it all came clear to her what was happening. Rhonda had gone back—all the way back to a previous lifetime. It had to be here that she started her love/hate relationship with carbohydrates. This was her chance to break the pattern that plagued her all the way from her earlier lives through to her present. She mustered up all of her courage, pulled her head back, looked her gentleman hunk straight in his beautiful hazel eyes, and said, "Frankly, my dear, I don't want a muffin."

In the split second, her plantation, her Southern charmer, and her muffins swirled around her in a blur of light and color, then they were gone with the wind. When Rhonda opened her eyes, she was back on the present-day leather couch, and Dr. Meyers was looking down at her, smiling.

"Oh, fiddle-de-de," muttered Rhonda as she struggled to sit up. It took her a few moments to pull herself together. Dr. Meyers waited patiently until she was ready to talk.

"So do you think you now have the power to resist carbohydrates?" she asked.

120

Rhonda couldn't quite recall what had just happened, but there was one thing she knew for sure. She was cured. "Yes!" she cried, smiling broadly. "Yes, I do! As God as my witness, I'll never eat carbs again!"

As she left the doctor's office, she walked down the street with a light step. She intentionally took the path that would pass the bakery, confident that she wouldn't stop in this time. She quickened her strides, and as she approached the door (and the wonderful smells emanating from inside), she amazed herself at how little it affected her. Then, to further prove that she was completely cured of her affliction, she decided she'd go inside and challenge herself to giving into temptation. Just as she was about to enter, however, a man she didn't see until the last second reached the door at the same time. He stopped short and gave her a slight bow, waving her to go ahead.

"Thank you," she said, and when she looked up, she saw an unbelievably handsome man. He looked strangely familiar, but she couldn't quite place him. He gave her a warm smile, and she couldn't help but returned it to him, whoever he was.

They walked together to the counter. "I hear they make the best pecan pie muffins this side of the Mason-Dixon," he said with a soft Southern drawl. "Would you allow me the pleasure of buying you one?"

Rhonda smiled. One muffin wouldn't hurt.

southern charm pecan muffins

121

orange you cute muffins

makes 12–15 muffins

1¾ cups flour

¼ cup sugar

2½ teaspoons baking powder

½ teaspoon salt

1 egg, beaten

¾ cup orange juice

⅓ cup salted butter, melted

½ cup orange marmalade

Streusel Topping:

2 tablespoons flour

2 tablespoons brown sugar

1 teaspoon cinnamon

1 tablespoon cold salted butter

1. Preheat oven to 400 degrees.

2. In a large bowl, mix together dry ingredients (flour through salt). Form a well in the center. Set aside.

3. In a separate bowl, mix together egg, orange juice, and melted butter. Pour into dry-ingredient well and stir until just moistened.

4. Lightly grease or paper-line muffin cups. Fill each cup ⅓ full of batter. Carefully spoon 1 tablespoon marmalade into center of each cup. Top with batter until cup is ⅔ full.

5. To make streusel topping, mix together flour, brown sugar, and cinnamon in a small bowl. Cut in cold butter using two forks or pastry blender until mixture crumbles. Sprinkle about a tablespoon of topping evenly over each muffin.

6. Bake 15 to 20 minutes or until a toothpick comes out clean. Cool 5 minutes before removing from pan.

Darin

Darin is adorable, and all you want to do is give him a fresh squeeze. Working in the orange groves has given him a body that is most a-peeling on the eyes. He's full of vitamin C, as well as vitamins S, T, U, and D. A day, or night, without Darin is like a day without sunshine.

candy man
muffins

makes about 12 muffins

2 cups flour

¼ cup sugar

¼ cup brown sugar

2 teaspoons baking powder

½ teaspoon baking soda

¼ teaspoon salt

⅓ cup salted butter, melted

1 egg, slightly beaten

¾ cup milk

1 teaspoon vanilla extract

1 cup dark chocolate chips

½ cup dried tart cherries,
coarsely chopped

1. Preheat oven to 375 degrees.

2. In a large bowl, mix together dry ingredients (flour through salt). Form a well in the center. Set aside.

3. In a separate bowl, mix together butter, egg, milk, and vanilla extract. Pour into dry-ingredient well and stir until just moistened. Fold in chocolate chips and cherries.

4. Lightly grease or paper-line muffin cups. Fill each cup ¾ full of batter. Bake 15 to 20 minutes, or until toothpick inserted in the center comes out clean. Cool 5 minutes before removing from pan.

if you like candy man muffins, then you'll love

Miles

Some like it spicy, but Miles likes it sweet. While he is known for his many confections, it's his devoted affection for you that makes him irresistibly complete. His unbearably sweet looks and sugar-coated charm make this candy man give you the ultimate sugar rush. And why not? If anyone can, the candy man can!

t-k-oatmeal muffins

makes about 12 muffins

1. Preheat oven to 350 degrees.

2. In a large bowl, mix together flour, ⅓ cup oats, and baking powder. Form a well in the center. Set aside.

3. In a medium skillet, heat butter, ⅔ cup oats, ¾ cup brown sugar, and cinnamon until lightly browned. Add water and ¼ cup brown sugar. Bring to a slow boil and cook about 5 minutes. Cool.

4. In a small bowl, whisk together milk and egg. Stir in raisins and let stand for 2 minutes.

5. Pour butter mixture and egg mixture into the dry-ingredient well, and stir until just moistened.

6. Lightly grease or paper-line muffin cups. Fill each cup ¾ full. Bake 20 to 25 minutes, or until a toothpick comes out clean. Cool 5 minutes before removing from pan.

1½ cups flour

⅓ cup quick oats

4 teaspoons baking powder

¼ cup butter

⅔ cup quick oats

1 cup brown sugar, divided

½ teaspoon cinnamon

⅔ cup water

1 cup milk

1 egg

1⅔ cups raisins

127

A Total Knockout

The shouts and groans from the living room could be heard throughout the house. It was the "Big Fight Night." Jack and Eva were hosting the neighborhood television viewing of the boxing match because they had the biggest television on the block. It was so large that it took up an entire wall of their entertainment room.

Eva should have realized, when her boyfriend insisted they purchase the monstrous television on the premise that they could invite friends and family over to view various programs in comfort, that what he really meant was she would be the one to provide the snacks and drinks for him and all his pals. She would also be the one to clean up the post-match, game, or play-off slop. Lucky me, she thought as she hid out in the kitchen, trying to avoid all the testosterone flying around the room, like a swarm of locusts on a feeding frenzy.

Eva rolled her eyes and reminded herself to make her friend, Marie, pay dearly for bailing on their planned "Girls' Night Out" as the guys noisily occupied her entertainment room. All hope of escaping the ritualistic male bonding had slipped away with Marie's phone call canceling their evening's plans. Strep throat was as good an excuse as any, but couldn't she have taken an aspirin or something and rested after their night out? Eva had to smile as she pictured her friend Marie, with a red congested nose, ordering a hot cup of tea, while Eva ordered herself a martini. Okay, she thought, I'm being selfish. Marie really did sound miserable when she'd called.

A sudden burst of cheers and hoots of joy resounded throughout the house. "I should have gone somewhere, anywhere, instead of hiding out here," she grumbled aloud in her empty kitchen, slamming dishes around in the sink. "But no, I get stuck at home to play caterer and maid to a bunch of middle-aged couch potatoes who couldn't care less if I was there or not, just so long as there was enough food and the right brand of beer to go around."

Eva was definitely feeling sorry for herself and unappreciated. She'd cleaned and catered for Jack and his friends, but it was Jack, who hadn't really lifted a finger, who was regaled with slaps on the back and punches in the arms in warm gratitude for so generously providing the right brand of "brewski" and "chow." Eva had actually snorted over those comments. She'd been the one to run around to the different markets trying to get everything she knew they liked. She had even made Jack's favorite oatmeal raisin muffins. Maybe she didn't want a slap on the

128

back of thanks, but would a simple "thank you" be too much to ask for? Obviously, it is, she thought, sighing out loud.

A sudden "Nooo!" was wailed almost in unison in the entertainment room. Eva rolled her eyes again. Then, her curiosity got the better of her and she took a peek around the corner to see what all the fuss was about. There, on the big screen, were two boxers. They looked like warriors of old. One was battered and bloody—obviously losing. When Eva focused on the victor, the image of him made her heart start to pound. He stood tall, like a god from an ancient battle. His muscles, over-defined and rippled, glistened with every move. There was nary a scratch on him save the beginning of a bruise around one eye. Every move he made was fluid, precise, and graceful, in a very masculine sort of way. Maybe boxing isn't so bad after all, Eva thought as she continued to watch the image on the big screen, mesmerized.

The bell that signaled the end of the round rang, and the camera zoomed in for a close-up view of the beaten boxer's face. God, that must hurt, Eva thought with pity and disgust. Suddenly, the screen changed to a beer commercial with young women clad in next to nothing, causing the room to erupt in loud hoots and howls of approval from the men in the room who had suddenly reverted into Neanderthals. This dis-play immediately brought Eva back to her senses, and she retreated to the safety of the kitchen.

She looked around at the mess made from all the effort of getting ready for Jack's "Boy Bonding" and cringed. She really wasn't in the mood to go another round with the dishes after already washing several loads earlier.

"Ugh!" she grumbled to the room in frustration. "One would think, after baking Jack's favorite muffins, he'd at least do the dishes." She grabbed a dish towel and started wiping off the counter when she suddenly stopped and tossed it aside. Who am I kidding? she lamented to herself. Why am I even surprised? Obviously the honeymoon phase of this relationship is well over. Eva let out a loud sigh and shouted in the direction of the entertainment room, "It's a good thing these muffins are my favorites, too, Mister!" Jack didn't reply. Eva reached to grab the last muffin off the cooling rack and bit into it. The sweet, moist, tantalizing flavor filled her mouth and she temporarily forgot about Jack, his Neanderthal buddies, and their stupid boxing match.

After she'd finished enjoying the delicious muffin, Eva resigned herself to the task of washing the rest of the dishes. She had to admit that the water felt good as she slipped her hands into the warm, soapy suds. Sighing, she leaned against the sink countertop

129

and stared out the kitchen window into the dark sky, watching a star twinkle in the cloudless night. Eva let the warm dishwater slowly cascade over her hands, and as she rested for the first time that day, she suddenly realized how incredibly tired she was. Closing her eyes for a moment, she let her mind wander . . .

"You're a knockout," a husky voice whispered from directly behind her.

He'd knock any girl's breath away with his "one, two" good-looks punch . . .

Startled, she whipped around. Warm, soapy water dripped down her arms and hands onto the kitchen floor as she stared, awestruck, into the incredibly handsome face of Dirk, the beautiful boxer from the big screen! He towered over six feet tall and every inch of him was pure perfection. His chiseled chest glistened, and his bulging muscles made her mouth water. He'd knock any girl's breath away with his "one, two" good-looks punch the moment they laid eyes on him, and Eva was definitely no exception.

"Wha . . . Excuse me?" Eva finally managed to stammer out as she tried not to choke on her own tongue.

I've got to be dreaming, she thought, and gave her head a very hard shake to bring herself back to reality.

"You're a knockout, Babe," he drawled out, lowering his gaze to give her the once-over. He smiled his approval at her.

Eva's legs threatened to give way to liquefaction, and her jaw dropped open at his intense perusal of her body. She suddenly felt totally undressed. Each and every spot on her body where his gaze lingered was burning, as if on fire. The room had quickly become very warm and closed in. Eva's head began to swim and she was finding it difficult to breathe normally.

"Who, me?" Eva asked in a voice that was just above a whisper, trying to get control of her breathing and her emotions that were quickly threatening to come undone.

"Yeah, you. You can be in my corner anytime," he answered, winking. He casually strutted to the kitchen table, pulled out a chair, and lazily sat back in it, as he brought his very large, bulging arms behind his head so that it could rest in his hands. Noticing that Eva was gawking at his magnificent build, he flexed his arm and gave her a sly, sexy smile.

"Oh . . . my . . . " Eva said shakily. Jack had a nice build, but there was no imaginable way he could compare to Dirk, the boxer, sitting stretched out before her. Every part of his body was a firm, solid muscle built to be worshiped. This guy is not one to throw a stick at, Eva thought to herself. She did, however, want to throw herself at him.

130

"I just saw you on television . . . " she began, as she began to question her sanity.

Dirk smiled and interrupted, "I know, that's why I am here."

"So . . . are you my imagination?" Eva questioned. This could be good, she thought, very good.

"Baby, I am anything you want me to be." Small tingles of excitement ran down Eva's back when he'd slowly annunciated the word "anything." "What's your pleasure?" he said with a wink.

"You're here just for me?" Eva squeaked out.

"Just for you," Dirk said softly as he looked directly into Eva's eyes with great intensity.

Eva's failing breath abandoned her altogether as it left her with a sudden whoosh at Dirk's firm confirmation. The possibilities were endless, and Eva had always had a very active imagination, thanks to all the steamy romance novels she'd been reading for years. Her extremely boring evening was finally starting to pick up some speed. And what speed it was!

Yes! Eva thought, as her mind started to race. Someone had taken notice of her, and this someone was gorgeous. If this was dementia, it wasn't so bad. In the past, her vivid imagination had taken her down some very embarrassing wrong turns. This time, it looked to be a grand adventure that Eva couldn't see any possible reason for not following where it led.

Dirk got out of the chair he'd been sitting in and came to stand directly in front of Eva. Lifting the dish towel off the counter, Dirk reached out, took Eva's hands into his large ones, and began to massage them dry. He began caressing each hand ever so slowly, in a very sensual way. He lingered on the palm of her hands and then began a slow, feather-light ascent of her body by tracing a serpentine line up her arms, shoulders, and neck. He massaged all the way up to her face where he came to a full stop to rest on her lips. Goodness, Eva fervently hoped, don't let me start drooling now.

"I'd like to go ten rounds with you," he said in a low voice that dripped with suggestiveness. He graced her with a lazy smile that dazzled her senses even further. Dirk raised one of her hands to his lips for a hot, wet kiss that ended with him nibbling the tips of her fingers. "What do you think?" he asked, looking up with smoldering eyes.

What did she think? What did she think? She was thinking right about then that she was going to have a heart attack after a little one-on-one sporty action with an exceedingly easy-on-the-eyes boxer.

Somewhere, somehow, in the last couple of minutes, the line between Eva's reality and fantasy blurred and her boxer boy had become real in every sense of the word. From the feel of the touch of his hand on her body, to the feel of his cool breath against her face, he was tangible.

Giving up any idea of returning to sanity, Eva reached up and encircled Dirk's neck with her arms, pulling him in the last bit of distance. Their bodies molded one another's as she knew they would. It was her fantasy, after all. They were a perfect fit. Slowly

132

Dirk brought down his lips toward Eva's waiting ones. She felt herself pucker with anticipation . . .

The sound of Jack's voice knocked Eva back to reality like a swift, solid upper cut. "I just came to check if we've got any more nachos? We're all out in there," he said, popping his head into the kitchen and pointing back toward his friends. Eva froze. "Honey, are you okay? Were you just . . . kissing the dish towel?" Jack asked slowly.

Gone. Just like that. Eva's vivid fantasy vanished with the reality of the Neanderthals' need for food. They'd interrupted her home and now she couldn't even have a decent fantasy without a cater call. Eva quickly dropped the towel and gave him a look that warned she was about to have a prize-winning fighting match against him of her own.

Jack knew the look well and he quickly stepped in the kitchen to calm her down. Wrapping his arms around her and hugging her tightly, he planted an affectionate kiss on the top of her head. It wasn't as romantic and steamy as Dirk's approach, but she had to admit it was nice.

"You know, Babe, I really appreciate you letting me and the guys watch the match, and all the work you put into making the guys and me comfortable. You spoil me, and I know I'm a pretty lucky guy."

Jack let her go and started grabbing more bags of chips from the counter. Opening the refrigerator, he called back. "Mmm, we're about out of beer. And, hey, can you make some more of those muffins?"

More muffins? Eva mused. "I'll make more muffins for you, Hon," she graciously offered, which, of course, had nothing to do with Dirk. Nah . . . nothing at all.

Jack stopped rummaging for other eatables long enough to poke his head above the fridge's door and smile up at her. "You're the best."

Before he had even left the kitchen, Eva was already going to get the flour. "Round two, coming up!"

t-k-oatmeal muffins

133

patriotic ★ muffins

makes 12–14 muffins

2½ cups flour

4 teaspoons baking powder

½ teaspoon salt

1 cup sugar

½ cup salted butter, melted

2 eggs, beaten

1 cup milk

1½ teaspoons vanilla extract

½ cup white chocolate chips

1 cup finely chopped
  maraschino cherries

1 cup fresh or frozen
  blueberries, slightly thawed

1. Preheat oven to 375 degrees.

2. In a large bowl, mix together flour, baking powder, and salt. Form a well in the center. Set aside.

3. In a separate bowl, stir together sugar, butter, eggs, milk, and vanilla until well blended. Pour into dry-ingredient well and stir until just moistened.

4. Pour one third of the batter into a small bowl. Gently fold in white chocolate chips.

5. Pour another third of the batter into a different small bowl. Gently fold in cherries.

6. In remaining third, gently fold in blueberries.

7. Lightly grease or paper-line muffin cups. Layer each cup with 1 tablespoon of the blueberry batter mixture, 1 tablespoon of the white chocolate chip batter mixture, then 1 tablespoon of the cherry batter mixture. Bake 15 to 20 minutes or until a toothpick comes out clean. Cool 5 minutes before removing from pan.

if you like patriotic muffins, then you'll love

Sammy

Sammy is ready, willing, and able to pledge his love to you. His one mission is to serve you, and you alone. He's true blue—and united the two of you will stand. After days of drilling, he's your lean, mean, loving machine. He pledges he'll never be AWOL, but he won't mind waving his white flag to surrender his heart to you.

afternoon tee muffins

makes 16 muffins

1. Preheat oven to 400 degrees.

2. In a large bowl, mix together dry ingredients (flour through nutmeg). Form a well in the center. Set aside.

3. In a separate bowl, stir together eggs, buttermilk, and butter. Pour into dry-ingredient well and stir until just moistened. Gently fold in raisins.

4. Lightly grease or paper-line muffin cups. Fill each cup ¾ full of batter. Bake 15 to 20 minutes or until a toothpick comes out clean. Cool 5 minutes before removing from pan.

1½ cups flour

1 cup sugar

½ teaspoon salt

1½ teaspoons baking powder

1 teaspoon baking soda

1½ tablespoons cinnamon

1 teaspoon nutmeg

2 eggs, beaten

1 cup buttermilk

1 tablespoon salted butter, melted

1½ cups raisins

Afternoon Tee Time

"Who decided golf was a fun sport?" Wendy mumbled to herself out of earshot of her girlfriends. It had only taken her one hour and thirteen strokes to reach her first green, and even though her friends were supportive and encouraging, she could tell that even they were getting annoyed.

Hit a little ball with a stick and chase it around the grass. Try to knock it into a hole. Wendy could think of better things to do with her afternoon, but her friends had pretty much forced her to join them and give golf a try. They even promised her there'd be cute golfers and pros everywhere. Yet looking around, the only guys she had seen were the ones that had started just ahead of them, and were now nowhere to be seen—a foursome of old men in polo shirts filled with beer bellies that flowed over the tops of their polyester pants. The Muffin Top Gang, she had silently labeled them upon first glance.

It took Wendy another four strokes to get the ball into the cup. Despite the cheers from her friends, she really wanted to call it a day. She couldn't imagine repeating this torture eight more times, but the girls would hear nothing of it. They all grabbed their bags and pulled her along to the next tee.

Halfway there, Wendy set her clubs down to take a break. Those puppies were a lot heavier than they looked! She wiped her face, removing the sweat and the last of her makeup, except for the mascara that ran partway down her cheeks. I'm sure I look like a pudgy Alice Cooper, she thought to herself, becoming increasingly cranky. How she wished she had been brave enough to wear shorts like her thin, cool friends, instead of sporting her heavy, nonbreathable pants, but she was way too self-conscious to do so. And no one told her that flip-flops weren't the appropriate shoe apparel on a golf course even though they worked just fine at the Putt-Putt Mini Golf.

"Go on ahead. I'll catch up," she called to her friends as she sat on the golf bag, sweating and rubbing her sore feet. Wendy watched as they walked down the path, laughing and talking. Finding her bottle of lukewarm water, she took a drink and looked around. She had to admit it was gorgeous out on the green. The golden rays of the afternoon sun blazed gloriously on the immaculately manicured grounds. The only sound, save the fading voices of her friends, was the wind rustling through the leaves of the giant oak trees that lined the links. No wonder people ditch work to go golfing, Wendy thought to herself. Forgetting the past hour of hell, she

138

found herself being lulled into a state of tranquility and peace. Closing her eyes, she took a deep breath.

From somewhere far off, a tiny voice reached her ear. "Fore!" However, in her revelry of the moment, it didn't quite register. Wendy remembered lazily thinking, do you yell out your score in golf? It wasn't until she heard her friends screaming at her to watch out that she realized her peril. She spun in the direction of the call, just in time to see an Intercontinental Ballistic Titleist bearing down on her head. She tried to duck, but it was too late . . .

When she opened her eyes, Wendy found herself sitting in a shiny white golf cart. She stepped out of it and onto the green, where her ball sat five feet from the hole. Somehow, the grass had become an impossibly rich shade of Kelly green, thick and lush under her dazzlingly white golf shoes. Wait, golf shoes? Suddenly, she realized that her bunchy pants had been replaced by an adorable short blue skirt that showed off her toned legs. On top was a sleeveless Argyle vest in pink and matching blue. Wendy had to admit, she made an adorable golfer.

"Nice lie," came a smooth voice, almost as if the wind brought it through the trees.

Wendy turned. There he stood, silhouetted by the green grass, looking like he just stepped out of the pages of a golf magazine. His designer clothes were impeccable, and from the cut of his pants to the lay of his shirt, it was very obvious that there wasn't a muffin top on this hunk. He was gorgeous. Her breath caught in her throat, loud enough for him to hear. He leaned against his golf club and smiled.

"Nice what?" she blurted out, her voice sounding strained.

His nearness flustered her beyond belief, and based on her heart rate, golf was suddenly becoming an aerobic sport.

"Your lie. You're in a desirable position . . . on the green. Your ball's so close to the pin," he said with grin that made her melt. "You don't need any wood on this one."

"I don't?" she sputtered.

"Well, I guess that's more your call," he said giving her a wink.

"I'm new at this," she blurted out.

"I'm Ace," he said, just above a whisper. "We should form a twosome. I can even give you a stroke or two, if you'd like . . . "

She tried to talk. Really, she did, but all she could do was mutely and vigorously nod.

He walked up to Wendy, his piercing blue eyes looking like they stole their color from the sky over his head. Without a word, Ace slid around behind her. Reaching around, he took both her hands in his. The touch of his arms along the length of hers sent a cascade of chills down Wendy's spine.

"First, you need to work on your grip," Ace whispered in her ear. "It should be firm, controlled." He tightened his hands over hers. Wendy just hoped her knees would hold up.

"Now, I'll help you find your sweet spot." Her breath quickened, and Ace gave a small chuckle. "It's the center point of the face on the club, and that's where you want to contact the ball," he murmured. "You'll know when you've found it. It'll feel good. Very good."

Wendy found herself having trouble focusing on the ball. "Next, the back swing. Pull back gently, turn at your waist, hip forward." Ace moved in closer, pressing his hip against hers. His nearness flustered her beyond belief, and based on her heart rate, golf was suddenly becoming an aerobic sport.

"Now," he whispered softly, "the most important part: the follow-through. I always make sure to finish completely."

Wendy tried to keep it together, but she choked—her body becoming jelly just as she swung the club. The ball rolled wide of the hole and continued off the green.

They stood, still pressed together, and watched the ball roll into the tall grass and out of sight. "That's the rough," he calmly chuckled.

"Rough's not good?" Wendy asked, forcing herself to try and think clearly.

"Well," he said slowly, "I guess that all depends . . . " He spun her around, never losing his hold.

Ace gazed at Wendy deeply with those mesmerizing eyes. Even though her body had stopped spinning, her head kept whirling around, and she closed her eyes. "Oh, I'm feeling so dizzy . . . " she moaned.

When Wendy opened her eyes again, she found herself flat on the grass. She looked up, and the view just about killed her. Standing over her and staring down were the faces of her worried girlfriends and the Muffin Top Gang.

"Are you all right?" one of her friends asked.

"What?" she mumbled. "Where's Ace?"

"Ice?" asked one of the old Muffin Top guys. "They have some in the clubhouse."

"Good idea," said a different Muffin Topper. "We can take the little lady there right now!"

Before Wendy knew what was happening, they scooped her up and put her in their cart. The four Muffin Top Gang members loaded in around her and

140

took off with a lurch.

"We'll meet you there!" yelled her friends, running to try and keep up with the overloaded vehicle.

With each bump of the cart, it felt as though Wendy's head would split apart at any second.

"Oh, Ace," she moaned.

"Almost there," reassured the guy next to her. "Hey, I bet we've got some ice left in the cooler, little lady!" He reached behind the seat and pulled out a chunk of melting ice. "Here you go," he said, handing the dripping mass to her. He looked back in the cooler. "What do you know, we still have muffins, too!"

"Muffins!" cheered the other three, and they each grabbed for one, devouring them like they hadn't seen food in days, which she knew couldn't be further from the truth.

Closing her eyes, Wendy held the ice to her throbbing, swimming head. Through her haze, she heard one of the guys offer her the last muffin. Never being able to pass up a yummy carbohydrate, even now with a possible concussion, she held out her hand, and he placed it on her palm. Wendy took a bite, and it was good. Sure, it filled her stomach, but it didn't fill the emptiness in her heart. It was as if a chamber had been damaged when Ace vanished . . . like there was a hole in one.

state fair corn dog muffins

makes 15–18 muffins

1½ cups flour

¾ cup cornmeal

¼ brown sugar, firmly packed

1 tablespoon baking powder

½ teaspoon salt

2 eggs, slightly beaten

1½ cups milk

1 cup grated cheddar cheese

9 hot dogs, cut into chunks

1. Preheat oven to 400 degrees.

2. In a large bowl, mix together dry ingredients (flour through salt). Form a well in the center. Set aside.

3. In a separate bowl, mix together egg, milk, and cheese. Pour into dry-ingredient well and stir until just moistened. Fold in hot dog chunks.

4. Lightly grease or paper-line muffin cups. Fill each cup ¾ full of batter. Bake 15 to 20 minutes, or until a toothpick inserted in the middle comes out clean. Cool 5 minutes before removing from pan.

if you like state fair corn dog muffins, then you'll love

Curtis

It's autumn and the colorful lights and mouth-watering smells arouse your senses and invite you to enjoy yourself at the state fair. Curtis graciously smiles and asks if you'd like to buy a corn dog from his stand. This absolutely gorgeous guy—in his tight, white T-shirt and form-fitting pants—is one fair attraction you could enjoy for hours. His eyes sparkle as he waits for your answer. You order one—then get back in line again for another. Curtis's body could win first prize in any state fair and you don't care how corny you have to be to get his undivided attention.

ain't that a peach muffins

makes about 12 muffins

2 cups flour

1 tablespoon baking powder

1/4 teaspoon baking soda

1/4 teaspoon salt

1/4 cup salted butter, melted

1 egg, slightly beaten

1 teaspoon vanilla extract

3/4 cup sour cream

1/2 cup milk

2 cups diced and peeled fresh peaches

streusel topping:

1 tablespoon salted butter, melted

2 tablespoons flour

2 tablespoon sugar

1/2 teaspoon cinnamon

1. Preheat oven to 350 degrees.

2. In a large bowl, mix together dry ingredients (flour through salt). Form a well in the center. Set aside.

3. In a separate bowl, mix together butter, egg, vanilla, sour cream, and milk. Gently fold in peaches. Pour into dry-ingredient well and stir until just moistened.

4. Lightly grease or paper-line muffin cups. Fill each cup 3/4 full of batter. Set aside.

5. For streusel topping, stir together all ingredients in a small bowl. Sprinkle evenly over batter cups.

6. Bake for 15 to 20 minutes, or until a toothpick inserted in the center comes out clean. Cool 5 minutes before removing from the pan.

144

if you like ain't that a peach muffins, then you'll love

Derek

Derek is your very own personal psychiatrist. With his impeccable white lab coat and inviting look, he makes you melt as you lie sprawled across his leather patient couch. He's guaranteed to make you feel just peachy at the end of your hour-long session. Simply sit back and relax as he works his way to the "pit" of your deepest problems . . .

sunny day muffins

makes 12 muffins

1. Preheat oven to 375 degrees.

2. In a large bowl, mix together dry ingredients (flour through salt). Form a well in the center. Set aside.

3. In a separate bowl, mix together lemon zest, egg, ¼ cup butter, and milk. Pour into dry-ingredient well and stir until just moistened.

4. Lightly grease or paper-line muffin cups. Fill each cup ¾ full of batter. Bake 15 to 20 minutes or until a toothpick comes out clean. Let cool 5 minutes before removing from pan.

5. For topping, brush tops of muffins with melted butter, then dip into sugar.

1¾ cups flour

½ cup sugar

1 tablespoon poppy seeds

2 teaspoons baking powder

½ teaspoon salt

1 tablespoon lemon zest

1 egg, beaten

¼ cup salted butter, melted

¾ cup milk

Topping:

2 tablespoons salted butter, melted

2 tablespoons sugar

147

Looking on the Bright Side

The first indication that something wasn't right was that little nagging feeling Amy always got in her gut just before something unpleasant was about to hit. She had woken up with that feeling, and by the time she'd gotten to work, it was driving her nuts. It hadn't helped matters that it had been raining nonstop for the past few days, and she'd been fighting a cold that she just couldn't shake.

The second indication something was amiss came in the form of a Post-it note left on her computer screen, telling her the office manager, Sheila, wanted to see her immediately.

Not today, thought Amy, as she grabbed the note, crumpled it, and shot it into the wastebasket.

"Unh-unh-uh," scolded her best friend, Dana, who had peeked over her cubicle wall just in time to see Amy ditch the Post-it. "Medusa wouldn't like that." Sheila had been deemed "Medusa" behind her back when she started wearing a long, jet-black dreadlock-style wig in an attempt to look young and hip. What it made her look like was a raisin in a really bad hairpiece.

"It's only a Post-it, for crying out loud," Amy replied nasally, as she dug in her workbag. She pulled out a box of tissues, a Thermos filled with hot tea, and what she called a Sunny Day muffin, made of lemon and poppy seeds. They always made her think of summer, so she had made a batch the night before while trying to heat up her little apartment and shake off the winter blues.

"I know that, but you know she wants everything shredded. Her paranoia knows no bounds," Dana quipped in her Southern drawl. "Oh, yummy! Is that one of your famous Sunny Day muffins?"

Amy ignored her friend's question, knowing it would lead to her mooching part of her muffin. "And it's getting worse," Amy added. "Last week I caught her listening to the conversations in the restroom while she was in one of the stalls."

Dana giggled, but then her smile vanished when she looked up to see Medusa heading straight in their direction. She quickly slid back down to her side. "Run, Bambi, run!" she said just loud enough for Amy to hear. "Oh, she looks ticked. What 'cha do this time?"

Amy didn't have a chance to answer, as Medusa reached her desk and stopped abruptly. "Ms. Thompson, my office. Now."

148

Medusa spun on her heels and marched back to her office, her crazy dreadlocks swinging wildly around her head. Amy stood up and feebly followed. As she passed Dana's desk, her friend called out, "Can I have your muffin if you don't come out alive?"

Amy kept walking and called back softly over her shoulder, "Touch it and die."

Dana just giggled again and whispered, "Good luck."

Amy reached Medusa's door and hesitated a moment before she worked up the nerve to enter the lion's den. Taking a deep breath, she stepped in. There, behind a cluttered desk, sat her thin, short, horse-faced boss. Without looking up, Medusa commanded, "Sit down, Ms. Thompson."

Amy quickly sat across from her boss in a soft leather chair trying to look alert, although all she wanted to do was sleep off her cold. The big window behind Medusa's desk held a bleak portrait of the weather outside. Amy watched as huge raindrops splattered against the glass. Amy sneezed, shook her head a bit, and told herself to focus.

After what felt like an eternity, Medusa looked up. "It's time for your yearly evaluation," she said, in her monotone, almost robotic voice. She tapped her fingertips together to make a triangle. "After going over our projected timeline for the completion of the third-quarter fiduciary statements with the new guidelines from the corporate office . . . "

Amy struggled to pay attention as Medusa droned on, but the words all morphed into blah, blah, blah.

She tried shifting in her seat and blinking hard. The rain got louder against the window. Pitter-patter, pitter-patter.

It took all of Amy's willpower to keep her head from hitting the desk. The cold medicine she'd taken that morning on an empty stomach wasn't helping matters, either. Her mind drifted as she stared straight ahead, mesmerized by the strange lullaby: Blah, blah, pitter-patter, blah, blah, pitter-patter. She closed her eyes.

Suddenly, her mind shifted into some sort of survival mode, and she was transported away from her bleak surroundings to a place that couldn't be more opposite—a sunny day, where the warm summer rays beat down upon her chilled body, to a place where she was surrounded by scantily clad California body builder look-alikes of the male persuasion . . .

"How's it hanging?" asked an energetic, inquisitive voice.

Amy's eyes fluttered open. There, before her, drifting lazily on a floating chair in the middle of a sparkling pool, was a tall, lean hunk wearing only what God gave him and a pair of board shorts. From what

149

Amy could see, every inch of his body was toned and tanned. Gone was Medusa, her heinous wig, and the dreary, wet weather outside. The only thing wet that she could see now was Cody, her California hunk.

After giving Amy a royal once-over, Cody raised his eyebrows. "Dude, you've got some righteous curves," he said, obviously impressed. "Like, your body's totally smokin'." He gave her the thumbs up.

Somewhere in the back of her mind, Amy kept hearing the voice of reason whisper that this was all just a fantasy . . . she didn't care.

"Am I—am I dreaming?" Amy stuttered. She looked down to see she was standing waist-deep in the pool, and she was now clad in a teeny-tiny string bikini she'd never have the guts to wear in public. *Of course, I'm dreaming*, she thought.

150

Cody reached for her hand. Gently taking it into his, he began kissing the tips of her fingers and said, "The only thing that looks like a dream around here is you, Babe. Want a ride?"

"I . . . I want to ride you," Amy stammered. "I mean, I want to ride with you, not on you . . . the chair—the pool chair—I want to ride with you on the pool chair." *What is coming out of my mouth?* she cringed.

Cody let out a husky laugh. "Don't sweat it, Babe. We can do it all."

"We can?" Amy asked, incredibly embarrassed by her lack of vocabulary at that moment.

Pulling Amy into his lap, Cody hungrily embraced her from behind with his strong swimmer's arms. Then he gently nudged her head with his and began to run tiny little kisses along the length of her neck. A soft purr escaped Amy's lips. Taking it as encouragement, Cody began to nibble on her earlobes, sending chills down her back, in spite of the heat from the beating sun.

Somewhere in the back of her mind, Amy kept hearing the voice of reason whisper that this was all just a fantasy, brought on by illness and a bad drug reaction. She didn't care. She, Amy Thompson, was purring, actually purring.

"Nothing I like better than two hot, wet bodies," Cody breathed into Amy's ear. His kisses started to travel down her neck to her shoulders. "Do you want me to stop?

"No! No!" Amy shouted.

Medusa suddenly appeared directly in front of Amy. "What do you mean you didn't file last month's report?" she hissed.

Eek!

"I . . . er . . . I . . . I didn't mean . . . what I meant . . . I . . . uh, I don't feel so . . . " Amy struggled to make sense. The room swam before her eyes.

Snapping her fingers in front of Amy's face, Sheila contorted in anger as she barked, "Are you even listening to me? Hello?"

Amy brilliantly picked that moment to pass out.

Medusa ran to her office door, her dreadlocks flapping every which way, and yelled out, "Dana! Ms. Thompson's decided to faint. Call 911 and bring some water in here. Quick!"

After reassuring Amy that it was only the flu, the paramedics told her to go home, get plenty of fluids, rest, and eat properly. Sadly, they made no mention of a pool float or a California babe. Even without medical training, Amy knew that would be the best prescription they could possibly give her.

As Dana helped Amy into a cab, she guiltily brought Amy's half-eaten muffin from behind her back and handed it to her.

"I really didn't think you'd want it after your meeting with Medusa," Dana confessed.

"That's okay, you can have it," Amy said, too exhausted to care. "I'm going home to dream . . . I mean, rest. I'll get another muffin at home."

As the cab pulled away from the curb, Dana was left to wonder about the huge, odd smile that crept across Amy's face.

movie and a pizza night muffins

makes 18 muffins

2¾ cups flour

1 tablespoon baking powder

1 can (10¾ ounces) condensed tomato soup, undiluted

¾ cup water

½ cup grated cheddar cheese

½ cup grated mozzarella cheese

¼ cup diced pepperoni

¼ cup Italian sausage, cooked, crumbled and drained

⅓ cup chopped green onions

2 tablespoons ripe olives

1 teaspoon Italian or dry pizza seasoning

1. Preheat oven to 350 degrees.

2. In a large bowl, mix together flour and baking powder. Form a well in the center. Set aside.

3. In a separate bowl, mix together soup, water, cheeses, pepperoni, sausage, onions, olives, and seasoning. Pour into flour mixture and stir until just moistened.

4. Lightly grease or paper-line muffin cups. Fill each cup ¾ full of batter. Bake 15 to 20 minutes or until a toothpick comes out clean. Cool 5 minutes before removing from pan.

152

if you like movie and a pizza night muffins, then you'll love

Caine

$\mathcal{C}$aine, the movie idol with machismo, is your man—your leading man. The love scenes you can create will be filled with plenty of action shots that will segue to passion's delight. There will be no playacting when he takes you in his arms. Yours will be an epic love story where only mature audiences are allowed.

once in a blue moon muffins

makes about 12 muffins

1. Preheat oven to 350 degrees.

2. In a large bowl, mix together dry ingredients (flour through salt). Form a well in the center. Set aside.

3. In a separate bowl, mix together butter, eggs, sour cream, and buttermilk. Pour into dry-ingredient well and stir until just moistened. Gently fold in blueberries.

4. Lightly grease or paper-line muffin cups. Fill each cup ¾ full of batter. Bake 15 to 20 minutes, or until a toothpick inserted in center comes out clean. Cool 5 minutes before removing from pan.

1 cup flour

¾ cup sugar

1 cup blue cornmeal

2 teaspoons baking powder

1 teaspoon salt

½ cup salted butter, melted

3 eggs, slightly beaten

1 cup sour cream

½ cup buttermilk

1 cup blueberries, fresh or frozen

155

Once in a Blue Moon

Kathleen honestly thought it was a good idea. She had given her parents a weeklong cruise to the Mexican Riviera for their fiftieth anniversary, and as a little treat for herself, she decided to go with them. It's not like it's their honeymoon, she reasoned with herself, so she was sure they wouldn't mind a chaperone of sorts. Secretly, she planned to spend most of the day with them like the dutiful daughter, then discreetly excuse herself in the evening (okay, call it what it really would be—she'd ditch them) for company of her own choosing.

She had seen pictures at the travel agent's office of young, smiling people dancing the night away in the ship's disco, and the romantic in her had automatically gone into overdrive. She could imagine herself as the woman in the poster with her dream man at her side, discovering new love and romance as they sailed off into the sunset together.

However, the moment she stepped foot onto the ship, she came to the realization that her plan was going to go horribly awry. As she looked around at the boarding passengers, she made a quick mental calculation and to her dismay, she found that her presence brought the average age down to only about sixty-five. She had never seen so many old people in one place in her entire life. While most were ambulatory (if you count shuffling as walking), some were in wheelchairs, and a good number of them dragged oxygen tanks behind them. She did not see one man under the age of fifty, as frantically as she searched. She didn't have anything against the elderly; it was just that her vision of dancing with someone with his complete set of original teeth was fading fast.

After about an hour on board, she learned why the ship was full of blue-hairs. Unbeknownst to her when she booked their passage, the International Society of Senior Ballroom Dancers had also booked the cruise for their annual convention. Thousands of dancers ranging in age from fifty-five to a hundred and five would fill her ship, her ship of new love and romance, leaving precious room for anyone remotely her age. Even her disco was going to be transformed into a formal ballroom, and for the next seven days the only dancing in there would be tangos and cha-chas. She planned on having a very stern talk with that travel agent when they returned.

As the first day progressed and Kathleen became restless she told herself that she could at least spend time with her parents. But to her shock, they ditched her after lunch, telling her that they wanted some alone time. As she watched her parents walk off hand-in-hand down the deck, she couldn't believe what was happening.

156

Her parents didn't show up for dinner, so there she sat, all dressed up and sitting alone at a table of elderly strangers. They smiled and made polite conversation, but she found she didn't have too much in common with people who were born in the first half of last century. She sat there, desperately willing her week on the Geriatric Love Boat to go by quickly.

Suddenly, her voyage got markedly better. Their waiter approached the table, and Kathleen's jaw just about landed in her bread plate. There, dressed in snug black pants and a white button-down shirt with a black cummerbund, stood her dream man. His jet-black hair was neatly combed back, framing his deeply tanned face. He had large, dark brown eyes that would crinkle a bit at the sides when he flashed his smile of very white teeth.

He started serving the salad at the opposite side of the table, and this gave Kathleen ample time to stare at him. Pathetically, she didn't do it very discreetly. This was partly due to the fact that he was the first man she'd seen that was in her age group, but mostly it was due to the fact that he was so amazingly handsome. It quickly became evident that he was aware of her gaze, and he gave her a quick smile from across the table. Rattled, Kathleen promptly knocked over her water, spilling it across the table and down the front of her dress.

He rushed over to her side and helped her pick up her glass. He pulled the towel off his arm and began mopping up her mess. As he leaned over her, she saw that his tag had the name Javier on it. "Thank you, Javier," she said, slightly embarrassed.

"My pleasure, miss," he said with a touch of seductiveness and a slight Spanish accent. He lightly rubbed the back of her shoulder, and she sat up abruptly, taken aback from his touch. He leaned in and whispered quietly in her ear. "If there is anything you need, just let me know." Right then, all she needed for him to do was refill her water glass, because her throat had gone suddenly dry. But if he gave her a moment, she was sure she could think of something else.

Javier finished helping her without another word, then returned to the other side of the table to finish serving. Kathleen watched as he flirted with the ancient woman across from her, touching her lightly on the shoulder and laughing with her. It was obvious that the woman thoroughly enjoyed the attention, and Javier seemed to be genuinely attentive, just like he had been with her. Kathleen suddenly began to question his actions toward her. Had he said those things to her because it was part of the script he probably repeated to all the women at his table, young or decrepit, on every single cruise? Was she just projecting her desperate need for romance onto a man who was simply being nice because it was part of his job description? She was just about to acquiesce that it had meant nothing when he caught her eye again.

157

This time the look he gave her was unmistakable. His smoldering eyes pierced hers, and she saw him pull the right side of his luscious lip into a seductive grin. This time she was sure: Hunky Javier wanted to give her more than a Caesar salad.

Kathleen had never been keen on big dinners, as she usually got filled up somewhere after the bread and between the salad and main course. But tonight, she was thankful that she was going to be getting seven courses, because that gave her seven chances to see Javier. She was even more thrilled when he served her dish, because each time he found a way to nonchalantly touch her somehow. He touched her on the hand and on her back, and once he maneuvered his body so that his thigh brushed her arm. If this continued, she wasn't sure she'd make it to dessert.

In fact, she didn't. When Javier brought her dessert plate of something gooey and decadent, he slipped a note under her napkin. She saw him do it, and looked at him, questioningly. All he did was gesture toward it with his head, and he was gone.

Her heart was pounding as she pulled the napkin and the note to her lap. With trembling fingers, she opened it: Lido Deck. She looked around, but he was nowhere to be seen. Suddenly, she wasn't hungry for dessert. She was hungry for something else, and it was wearing a waiter's outfit.

"Excuse me," she asked the old man in the polyester leisure suit next to her. "Do you know how to get to the Lido Deck?"

"Sure, honey," he answered. "Up those stairs, out the double doors, and to the left. It's right by the disco." He leaned in, leering a bit. "They're having the fox-trot competition in there tonight. Want to join me?"

Kathleen quickly got up and was moving before the answer was completely out of her mouth. "Thanks, but no."

The tables were close together, so she had to squeeze her way past a few of the chairs. She was just about to make it to the aisle when the old woman across the table grabbed her arm and motioned her to come closer. Although Kathleen was in a hurry, she decided not to be rude.

The old woman smiled and looked at her with twinkling eyes full of wisdom. "Life's too short," she said to Kathleen. "Some chances only come along once in a blue moon."

Kathleen wasn't quite sure what she was talking about, but she smiled and thanked her. Quickly, she made her way through the dining room then followed the old man's directions to the Lido Deck. She looked around, but Javier was nowhere to be seen.

She walked out to the railing and leaned against it, taking in the cool night ocean air. She could hear the strains of an old song from the forties wafting from the disco. While she had wished it could have been the pounding beat of a great dance song, she had to admit that music was rather romantic. Closing her eyes, she could imagine swaying to the slow rhythm of a full orchestra.

She must have imagined too well because she began swaying out on the deck all alone. Without a sound, her body melded with another; a large, solid body that effort-

158

lessly fell into the rhythm of her sway. Her eyes fluttered open in surprise and found Javier a mere inches from her face.

"May I have this dance?" he asked, smiling and still swaying.

"I believe you already have it," she answered playfully. He pulled her closer to him and she could now feel that he was as strong and solid as he looked. She let her hands caress his back as she marveled at her boldness. She didn't even know this man, but everything felt so good, so right.

"My name's Kathleen, by the way," she said into his neck. She figured he should at least know who was groping him.

"I know," he said. "Kathleen Sullivan. You're from Tacoma, Washington, and you're here with your parents."

She pulled away a bit and looked at him, a little taken aback. He laughed softly. "Don't worry—I'm not a stalker or anything. I saw you when you boarded and then I asked around. This boat is like a small town; you get to know everyone and everything."

The music stopped and they moved apart, but not by much. All she wanted to do was stand and stare at this beautiful man who went to so much trouble to find out who she was. She hoped she would have the chance to find out all about him, as well.

"Wait right here. I'll be back in a moment," he said abruptly, squeezing her hands and then letting go to disappear into a side pantry-like room. He came back with both hands behind his back and with the biggest smirk anyone could have across his face.

"You didn't eat your dessert, so I thought you'd like this," he said, producing a perfect blueberry muffin atop one of the ship's fine china plates he had brought up from the kitchen. "Take a bite. It's our famous Blue Moon Muffin."

Kathleen's eyes grew wide and she clasped her hands together excitedly. But then she thought, Wait. Blue Moon? Wasn't that what the old woman said? She decided it was fate and took a big bite. Of course, it was delicious. She broke it in half to share with him and then they flirtatiously licked each other's fingers.

When the muffin was finished, Javier gently placed his hand under Kathleen's chin, tilting it up so all she could see were his beautiful eyes. He stared at her like no one had ever done before. She could feel his intensity clear to her core. "I know we just met, but I've got this feeling that there might be a chance for something . . . incredible." He kissed her softly, with the promise of more to come.

A new song began in the disco. "May I have this dance, as well?" Javier asked. She nodded and they fell back into each other's arms, swaying together in the cool, moonlit night. The singer began crooning the lyrics, and Kathleen couldn't believe her ears.

"Blue moon, you saw me standing alone . . ."

She smiled, holding on tight to her big, handsome new man and thanked her lucky stars for going on that once-in-a-lifetime trip.

159

say "cheese" muffins

makes about 12 muffins

2 cups flour

½ cup sugar

1 tablespoon baking powder

½ teaspoon salt

¼ cup salted butter, melted

2 eggs, slightly beaten

1 cup grated sharp cheddar cheese

½ cup grated mozzarella cheese

½ cup grated jack cheese

½ cup milk

1 cup sour cream

1. Preheat oven to 375 degrees.

2. In a large bowl, mix together dry ingredients (flour through salt). Form a well in the center. Set aside.

3. In a separate bowl, mix together butter, eggs, cheeses, milk, and sour cream. Pour into dry-ingredient well and stir until just moistened.

4. Lightly grease or paper-line muffin cups. Fill each cup ¾ full of batter. Bake 15 to 20 minutes, or until toothpick inserted in middle comes out clean. Cool 3 minutes before removing from pan.

160

if you like say "cheese" muffins, then you'll love

Jared

Jared doesn't need props to make his subjects smile at his photography studio. He's a first-class professional behind the lens, and one look at his sparkling eyes and flash-bulb grin makes all of his models feel right at home. Go ahead . . . what are you waiting for? You know you want to strike a pose in the presence of such great talent. Together, the two of you can create a gorgeous masterpiece. Say "Cheese"!

beer fest muffins

makes 12–15 muffins

2 cups flour

1 tablespoon baking powder

1 teaspoon salt

2 tablespoons sugar

1 egg, slightly beaten

6 ounces beer (allow to stand at room temperature and become flat)

1. Preheat oven to 350 degrees.

2. In a large bowl, mix together flour, baking powder, salt, and sugar. Form a well in the center. Set aside.

3. In a separate bowl, mix together egg and beer. Pour into dry-ingredient well and stir until just moistened.

4. Lightly grease or paper-line muffin cups. Fill each cup ¾ full of batter. Bake 15 to 20 minutes, or until toothpick inserted in center comes out clean. Cool 5 minutes before removing from pan.

if you like beer fest muffins, then you'll love

Hans

Hans brings new meaning to a six-pack of beer. With his six-pack abs and beautiful blue eyes, he is sure to take care all of your "ale-ments." This is one gentlemen's lager that can be poured into your heart, enrich your daily menu, and raise your spirits in no time at all. Three cheers for Hans!

lunch is served muffins

makes about 12 muffins

1. Preheat oven to 350 degrees.

2. In a food processor or blender, puree all ingredients until well blended.

3. Lightly grease or paper-line muffin cups. Fill each cup ¾ full with batter. Bake 25 to 30 minutes or until browned. Cool 5 minutes before removing from pan. Serve warm.

1 can (6 ounces) boneless and skinless salmon, undrained

2 eggs

¼ cup chopped celery

¼ cup chopped onion

½ cup quick cooking oats

½ cup flour

1½ teaspoons baking powder

¼ cup evaporated milk

2 teaspoons lemon juice

1 teaspoon salt

¼ teaspoon black pepper

1–2 drops hot sauce

165

Lunch Is Served

Olivia's day had started off like any other frantic weekday morning. First came the droning wail of the alarm clock, followed by the frenetic rush to get her husband and children washed up, dressed, fed, and off to meet their various buses on time. The only variation in this morning's routine had been the advent of a rainstorm that had begun in the early hours of the day. It didn't seem possible that a few tiny drops of water could cause such a fuss, but it had. Rain boots and umbrellas that hadn't been used since the last rainy season had to be sought out in a desperate search-and-rescue mission before anyone was able to set foot out the front door.

With book packs and lunchboxes in tow, followed by the ritual goodbye kisses, her family set off for their busy day. Olivia waved with a cheery smile from inside her nice, dry living room, watching her family make their final mad dash to their various destinations.

After seeing her last child step up into the school bus, Olivia stepped away from the front window and went to survey the remains from the morning chaotic rush. As she stood in the kitchen's doorway, she realized it was worse than she'd thought. Everything lay where her family had abandoned it. Somewhere between the demands for help with a stray shoe, misplaced homework, and an unsigned progress report, nothing seemed to have made it back to its proper place within the kitchen.

Half-finished glasses littered the table alongside some soggy cereal bits that floated in partially finished bowls of milk. Through tired eyes, Olivia glanced over the area. There was no doubt about it, the kitchen was a wreck. Thank goodness, she thought to herself, at least the mad morning rush was over.

While looking about the scattered remains of breakfast, her spirit brightened. There was a saving grace; they had left her a single muffin! She took a slow drink from her now cold cup of coffee and reached with anticipation for the muffin. She closed her eyes and bit into the moist, tender muffin. Heaving a contented sigh, Olivia's mind began to wander . . .

"Can I get anything for you?" came a smooth, silky voice.

Olivia turned instinctively toward the direction of the voice. There, before her stood every woman's fantasy, Gibson, Butler-Extraordinaire. He was tall, lean, dark, and handsome. He had broad shoulders, and he was built to please both in the kitchen and out of it. There

166

was a mysterious masculine energy about him and his eyes twinkled as he gave Olivia a sexy smile. "Your muffins are so moist and fluffy," he said with a grin.

Olivia lowered her eyes and gave his body a thorough look-over. She licked her lips and gave a sigh of satisfaction. Every inch of his body pleased her senses, from the crown of his head to tips of his toe. Add the fact that he also cleaned, and it just about put Olivia into a frenzy. Any man who could wield a cleaning tool was next to a god.

Life was wonderful. He was wonderful. She gave a sly grin as she began to think of everything she would love for him to do with a mop and a broom, and that was just for beginners. Later, when he was done with the house, he could move on to tasks of a more personal nature.

He tilted his head and asked in a husky voice, "Would you like me to butter your muffin?" It was like he could read Olivia's mind.

"Ohhh, yes!" she answered without a moment's hesitation. Her lips parted in anticipation.

She felt her heart beginning to beat wildly as he advanced toward her. His warm, strong hands clasped Olivia's and he slowly pulled her toward him. As she looked up, her eyes locked with his dreamy brown ones, and Olivia's breath caught in her chest. The sensation she was feeling caught her totally by surprise, and she audibly gasped. Still clasping Olivia's hand tightly, he very gently began to butter her muffin. A bit of butter touched the tip of her fingers, and he could not resist the temptation to raise her hand toward his lips.

"Let me get that," he boldly said, and began to lick off the creamy butter, then he moved on to nibbling the tip of her fingers.

"Thank you," Olivia whispered breathlessly. Each nerve ending was quivering with the excitement of his nearness.

Looking into her eyes, he whispered, "How may I serve you next?"

He was so close she could feel his warm, sweet breath on her. He smelled of spices and if she wasn't mistaken, a hint of Pine Sol. Her coffee was warming back up from the heat that was coming off the lusty gaze he was giving her.

Gibson raised the buttered muffin up to Olivia's lips and offered her a bite. Closing her eyes, Olivia bit into the muffin's rich moistness and gave a small moan of delight. Like an aphrodisiac, the muffin tantalized the senses.

When she opened her eyes, Gibson stared directly into hers and said, "You have a bit of butter on your mouth."

He did not give Olivia a second to respond. Gibson seized the moment to pull her into his big strong arms

167

for a complete embrace. Body touching body, Olivia felt she would soon become overwhelmed by the heat and consumed by her passion's desire.

"Let me get that for you," he said as he drew his face very close to hers. With a slow thrust of his tongue, he sensually licked the side of her lips to remove the offending butter. "I knew you'd taste delicious," he said. His voice was low and sultry.

> **Tiny little bursts of heat erupted where his lips touched, and Olivia now understood what people meant when they spoke of passion's fiery burn.**

"Really?" questioned Olivia.

"Yes," Gibson slowly replied while he nodded his head ever so slightly in agreement. Then he brought his lips down onto her for a slow, ravaging kiss.

Olivia's lips parted involuntarily and Gibson deepened his kiss. It was the nectar of the gods, and Olivia feasted in its sweetness, savoring each delicious sensation that her body felt, quickly becoming a quivering mass of need.

"I beg your pardon, madam, but I just couldn't help myself." Gibson said as he gave a slight shrug of his shoulders. "I've wanted to pull you into my arms the moment I saw you standing there. Your husband must be a very lucky man to wake up beside you every morning and go to bed with you every night. I would love to be able to hold you in my arms every night," then adding with a husky laugh, "along with all the other things I'd love to do to you, that is, if it so pleased you."

Gibson pulled her close to himself and rained tiny kisses on the top of her head, then began a descent downward. It felt wonderful to Olivia as she felt his buttery soft kisses trace a path along the face, neck, and shoulder area. Tiny little bursts of heat erupted where his lips touched, and Olivia now understood what people meant when they spoke of passion's fiery burn.

As far as Olivia was concerned, no explanation was required. That he found her desirable was more than enough. She, herself, felt the very same thing for him. Olivia's eyes misted over with the knowledge that here was a man who wanted her as a woman and not for missing shoes or stray briefcases. She wanted to luxuriate in his warm embrace forever.

"I won't make any excuses for my actions. I want you. It's that plan and simple."

His voice was ragged with emotions. "There's so much I want to do to you, but as your personal butler,

168

I have to ask, how may I further pleasure you?"

All her life she had waited for a handsome man to ask her what he could do for her, and now it was finally happening. Every woman should be faced with such a decision, she thought to herself with a smile. So what if it was a dream? She wanted to ride it to the end, wherever that might be. The raw, hungry sensation that began to burn inside her had absolutely nothing to with food and everything to do with the man who was holding her tightly.

For a split second Olivia couldn't decide if she wanted Gibson to take care of the kitchen with all its dirty dishes, or have him take care of her. It was an easy answer, she thought as her smile turned into a wicked grin. He could always do the dishes later. Duh!

"I want you to . . . " she began breathlessly.

In the distance she heard the sound of her front door opening and her husband calling out to her.

"Sweetie, it's just me," he called from the living room. "I forgot to take Jerry's new cell number with me when I left. I already called the office to let them know I'm running late." The sound of rustling papers was quickly followed by the sound of a glass breaking.

Olivia suddenly felt the release of her person from Gibson's embrace. He was gone . . . and he hadn't gotten around to cleaning the mess.

"Wait!" she called out in silent frustration. "Don't go."

Her husband popped his head into the kitchen and said, "Oh, Honey, I love you, too, but I've got a big presentation due at the end of the week. I promise, we'll spend more time together next week." He kissed her cheek and continued, "I broke a glass. Can you get it, Hon?"

He didn't even wait for an answer as he headed out the door, calling out behind him that he'd probably be home late, leaving Olivia standing with her cold cup of coffee in a messy kitchen all alone.

Looking thoughtfully at the paper wrapper that had held her muffin, she hit upon a brilliant idea. Maybe she would bake more muffins. It was cold and wet outside, and baking always heated up the house.

pick of the crop muffins

makes about 12 muffins

2 cups flour

¾ cup sugar

2 teaspoons baking powder

½ teaspoon salt

2 eggs, slightly beaten

1 cup milk

½ cup sour cream

¼ cup salted butter, melted

¾ cup chopped dried apricots

2 teaspoons orange zest

1. Preheat oven to 375 degrees.

2. In a large bowl, mix together dry ingredients (flour through salt). Form a well in the center. Set aside.

3. In a separate bowl, mix together egg, milk, sour cream, and butter. Fold in apricots and orange zest. Pour into dry-ingredient well and stir until just moistened.

4. Lightly grease or paper-line muffin cups. Fill each cup ¾ full of batter. Bake 15 to 20 minutes, or until toothpick comes out clean when inserted in the center. Cool 5 minutes before removing from pan.

170

Sonny

It's a cold fall morning. Sonny gives new meaning to the words "pick of the crop." As his lean, muscular body tends to the land, you can't help but wonder what it would be like for him to tend to your needs as well. Have no fear. You can be sure that when his long day is done, he'll be picking you to share his nights with.

triple-play muffins

makes about 12 muffins

1. Preheat oven to 350 degrees.

2. In a large bowl, mix together dry ingredients (flour through salt). Form a well in the center. Set aside.

3. In a separate bowl, stir together egg, yogurt, vanilla extract, and butter. Pour into dry-ingredient well and stir until just moistened.

4. Gently fold in all three types of chocolate until just blended.

5. Lightly grease or paper-line muffin cups. Fill each cup ¾ full of batter. Bake 15 to 20 minutes, or until a toothpick comes out clean. Cool 5 minutes before removing from pan.

1½ cups flour

½ cup sugar

1½ teaspoons baking powder

¼ teaspoon baking soda

¼ teaspoon salt

1 egg, slightly beaten

1 cup low-fat vanilla yogurt

1 tablespoon vanilla extract

⅓ cup salted butter, melted

¼ cup semisweet chocolate chips

¼ cup milk chocolate chips

¼ cup white chocolate chips

173

An Out of the Park Home Run

Her husband rushed into the kitchen. "Honey, have you seen my cleats?" It was Saturday morning, and the Ritual of the Weekend Athlete was in full tilt. Dressed in his gray, eternally grass-stained sweats, he dug through the pile of discombobulated shoes in the corner. It wouldn't be long before he left her at home so he could spend the day playing baseball with his friends, as they bonded, sweated, and overextended a myriad of muscle groups.

"Got 'em!" He gathered the rest of his bulky gear and awkwardly came toward her to plant a brusque kiss on her lips. "See you later," he said hurriedly as he bolted out the door. She gave him a half-hearted wave that he didn't see. And then he was gone. Again. Like any good sports widow, she sat in the kitchen like yesterday's news nursing a cup of tea and a bruised ego. She had already made three dozen muffins for the pot-luck at work, and she was trying to think of something to do while she waited for his game to end. She began to

imagine herself in a sexy negligee giving a "Come and get me, Big Boy" look to her husband when he got home, in an attempt to capture his interest. Immediately she realized the fantasy was totally wrong, and she switched the negligee for a sports jersey of his favorite team, and for good measure, she added a plate of his favorite snack, her decadent triple-chocolate muffins.

She sighed heavily and rolled her eyes toward the ceiling as she reached for one of the moist muffins left cooling on the counter. Men, she thought, shaking her head. She closed her eyes and bit into the dark, creamy richness, letting her mind drift at will.

"You could score a home run with those muffins of yours," came a deep, sultry voice.

Her eyes flew open. "I beg your pardon?" she stammered, as she found herself looking into the most beautiful, big, brown eyes she'd ever seen.

He was Chet Daniels, professional baseball's most sought-after player. He was tall and put together nicely, very nicely. He leaned his elbow across the countertop and propped his head into his hand as he gave her a wicked grin. His uniform, crisp, clean, and sparkling white, hugged him in all the right places. Physically, this man was blessed more than any man should be. Just looking at him made her toes curl.

174

Is this for real? she wondered to herself, praying that it was.

His thick brown hair fell across his face as he slightly lowered his head and gazed directly into her eyes. Without thinking, and pulled as if controlled by an outside power, she brushed back the stray lock. He gave a small, throaty laugh just before he spoke.

"I said: Those muffins look really good . . . moist, firm."

His voice was just above a whisper—low, sexy, and dripping with suggestiveness. He ran his index finger in a circular motion across the muffin she had bitten. Then he ever so slowly brought his fingers to his lips and tasted it. "Just as I imagined. Delicious."

He crossed to the other side of the counter where she sat mesmerized, and stood behind her. He clasped her waist from behind and drew her close. Tilting his head, he whispered in her ear. "We could make a great team . . . you and I. Trust me, I know how to play infield and outfield. There'll be no strike-out," he promised. She could feel herself blush a deep shade of crimson. "What do you say . . . want to play ball?"

She didn't even stop to think. Come to mama! Her head raced as it tried to catch up to her heart.

"I would love to play," she breathed, eagerly.

Within a split second, reality came crashing back and her dream man vanished like mist, blown away by her husband's resounding voice as he burst back into the kitchen. "Forgot my lucky bat!"

As he ran past, he stopped in his tracks when he noticed the plate of muffins. "Oh boy, Honey! Are those muffins for the team?"

She quickly reasoned murdering her husband was not an option, as she looked terrible in stripes. Besides, she thought to herself, I guess I can always make more!

"Sure, Sweetie," she cooed. "Oh, and feel free to play a double-header today."

He paused, scrunched his face, and smiled at his understanding wife. "You're the best!" he exclaimed and pecked her on the cheek as he scooped up the goodies and ran out the door.

She smiled to herself. Yes, yes I am, she thought. And I'm going to need a lot more muffins, too.

nightcap muffins

makes 15 muffins

2 cups flour

¼ cup sugar

2 teaspoons baking powder

½ teaspoon salt

1 teaspoon nutmeg

1 cup buttermilk

¼ cup salted butter, melted

1 egg, beaten

1 teaspoon rum extract

Topping:

¼ cup salted butter, melted

¼ cup sugar

½ teaspoon cinnamon

½ teaspoon nutmeg

1. Preheat oven to 375 degrees.

2. In a large bowl, mix together dry ingredients (flour through nutmeg). Form a well in the center. Set aside.

3. In a separate bowl, stir together buttermilk, ¼ cup melted butter, egg, and rum extract. Pour into dry-ingredient well and stir until just moistened.

4. Lightly grease or paper-line muffin cups. Fill each cup ¾ full of batter. Bake 15 to 20 minutes or until a toothpick comes out clean. Cool 5 minutes before removing from pan.

5. For topping, place melted butter in a shallow bowl. In a separate shallow bowl, mix together sugar, cinnamon, and nutmeg. Dip muffin tops first into butter, then dip in sugar mixture. Serve warm with butter.

176

if you like nightcap muffins, then you'll love

Gates

Gates is a man of sophistication. At the end of a long winter's day, he'll take off his three-piece suit and put on a smoking jacket made of fine red silk with black satin lapels. Then, he'll sit you down in front of a fire and want to hear about your day, your life, and your dreams as he shares a nightcap muffin with you. It might be a cold night, but Gates will warm your heart better than the finest brandy.

 # here comes the ice cream man muffins

makes about 12 muffins

1½ cups flour

2½ teaspoons baking powder

¾ teaspoon salt

2 tablespoons cold salted butter

2 cups strawberry ice cream, very soft

1 egg, slightly beaten

1. Preheat oven to 375 degrees.

2. In a large bowl, mix together dry ingredients (flour through salt). Using a pastry blender or two forks, cut in butter until mixture is crumbly. Form a well in the center. Set aside.

3. In a separate bowl, whisk together ice cream and egg. Pour into dry-ingredient well and stir until just moistened.

4. Lightly grease or paper-line muffin cups. Fill each cup ¾ full of batter. Bake 15 to 20 minutes, or until toothpick inserted in the middle comes out clean. Cool 5 minutes before removing from pan.

if you like say here comes the ice cream man muffins, then you'll love

Jack

The bells on the local ice cream truck ring differently today. The regular ice cream man called out sick and a new ice cream guy is in town. You wonder how a grown woman can get a cool treat without looking foolish. Aw, heck! Throwing caution to the nonexistent wind, you order a strawberry cone. Jack smiles and says the delicious dessert is on him—but soon enough it's on you. While flirting, he manages to melt your heart and the cone that's slowly dripping down your fingers . . .

naughty and nice eggnog muffins

makes 15 muffins

2¼ cups flour

1 teaspoon baking soda

1 teaspoon baking powder

1½ cups sugar

1 teaspoon ground nutmeg

¼ cup salted butter, melted

1¼ cups milk

2 eggs, beaten

2 tablespoons instant vanilla pudding mix

½ teaspoon vanilla extract

1. Preheat oven to 350 degrees.

2. In a large bowl, mix together dry ingredients (flour through nutmeg). Form a well in the center. Set aside.

3. In a separate bowl, whisk together butter, milk, eggs, pudding mix, and vanilla extract. Pour into dry-ingredient well and stir until just moistened.

4. Lightly grease or paper-line muffin cups. Fill each cup ¾ full of batter. Bake 15 to 20 minutes or until a toothpick comes out clean. Let cool 5 minutes before removing from pan.

if you like naughty and nice muffins, then you'll love

Klaus

Klaus has been working out this year. Gone is the bowl-full-of-jelly belly, and in its place is a rock-hard six-pack. His upper body is smoking, too, as he's been bench-pressing reindeer all summer long. Now he'll be able to slide down your chimney a lot easier. If you've been really good, he'll let you sit on his lap and tell him what you want. Ho, ho, ho-my-goodness!

mardi gras muffins

makes 12 muffins

1. Preheat oven to 400 degrees.

2. In a large bowl, mix together dry ingredients (flour through thyme). Form a well in the center. Set aside.

3. In a separate bowl, stir together eggs, buttermilk, sour cream, pimiento, green onion, and butter. Pour into dry-ingredient well and stir until just moistened.

4. Lightly grease or paper-line muffin cups. Fill each cup ¾ full. Bake 15 to 20 minutes, or until toothpick comes out clean.

1½ cups flour

½ cup yellow cornmeal

1 tablespoon sugar

1 tablespoon baking powder

1 teaspoon salt

½ teaspoon baking soda

½ teaspoon chili powder

½ teaspoon cayenne pepper

¼ teaspoon garlic powder

¼ teaspoon dried oregano

¼ teaspoon paprika

¼ teaspoon dried thyme

2 eggs, slightly beaten

¾ cup buttermilk

½ sour cream

¾ cup chopped pimiento

¼ cup finely chopped green onion

¼ cup salted butter, melted

A Mardi Gras Mystery

She only had herself to blame. In a moment of panic as a milestone birthday approached, Melissa had sat down and made a list of all the things she wanted to do before she died. Somehow, she thought experiencing Mardi Gras in New Orleans was important enough to earn a spot near the top. But now, as she stood in a steamy sea of drunken humanity, shoulder to shoulder with some very exuberant revelers who had spilled warm beer down the back of her shirt, she wondered if it was too late to remove this idea from her list and replace it with quiet high tea in England.

She and her boyfriend, Nate, had ventured out into the mob in an attempt to walk the couple of blocks to Bourbon Street, but in three hours had only managed to go less than half a block. "This is crazy!" she shouted to Nate, who stood close by but still had trouble hearing her over all of the commotion.

"Yeah! I can't even get to a beer!" he yelled back. "Stay here. I'm going to try to make it over there and get us some." He gestured to a little bar across the street, next to a bakery.

"Bring me something to eat, a muffin or something!" she called out as he wedged his way through a throng of dancing celebrants and out of sight. Melissa hadn't had anything to eat since the plane ride, and that complimentary bag of peanuts and half a drink had lost their staying power hours ago. An uneasy feeling of lightheadedness started creeping in as the mass of people flowed into the space Nate left behind.

Melissa told herself she should at least try to enjoy this once-in-a-lifetime experience, because she never, ever planned to do this again. Looking around, she had to admit it was an amazing sight. Bright buntings and flags decorated the balconies of all the buildings. Thousands of people packed the street. Many of them were in costumes; some crazy and irreverent, like the guy with the full beard and mustache in the Elvis/mermaid get-up. Others were extremely ornate and beautiful with sequins and too many feathers too count. It made Melissa wonder if there was a bunch of bald birds somewhere.

Then, of course, there were the beads. Every neck boasted strands of blues, purples, golds, and greens in a wide range of sizes, from tiny to baseball-sized. She wanted some, but the only offers she had received were from drunken male partygoers, who tried to en-

184

tice her to flash her bosom in exchange for a strand of beads—a Mardi Gras tradition she found too sleazy for her taste. She passed on their offers, not feeling the need to lift her shirt just to procure a cheap plastic necklace. *Typical males, all of them*, she thought. She figured she could wait for the parade that would be coming by soon, where they just threw the beads to the crowd, and it didn't matter if your shirt was up around your ears or not.

Melissa kept glancing back in the direction of the bakery, hoping to catch a glimpse of Nate bringing the much-needed sustenance, but being rather short, she had trouble seeing past the mob, which kept growing incredibly as the street continued to fill. Suddenly, over the cacophony, she heard someone on a loudspeaker. Looking toward the voice, she saw a New Orleans police officer on a horse addressing the crowd.

"Please move back to the curb!" he bellowed as his horse slowly plowed its way down the packed street. "Parade's starting in ten minutes! Please move back!"

The crowd cheered and began pressing away from the street and even closer around Melissa. "You've got to be kidding," she said aloud, but no one else seemed to care. They were having way too much fun to worry about one squished woman.

The mob had closed in so tightly around Melissa that someone was now pressed along her right side, and someone had his backside jammed against hers. "Excuse me," she said meekly to her new Siamese twin against her side. "Could you please move over?" But she couldn't be heard, because at that precise moment, the group in front of her suddenly had the need to sing something loud and unintelligible.

The body heat, the humidity, the overpowering smell of old beer, and her empty stomach proved to be a very bad combination, and Melissa's head spun. Mardi Gras morphed into a swirling sea of colors, smells, and sounds. She tried with all her might to keep it together, but she felt her body lurch—and then everything went dark.

Suddenly, Melissa felt herself rise, supported by two strong hands. A cool breeze hit her face as she struggled to open her eyes. At first, all she could make out was a blur of shiny colors and odd shapes. Shaking the cobwebs and breathing deeply, her surroundings slowly came into focus, and she could now make out a beautiful mask covering what looked like a beautiful face on a beautiful man standing over her. He was tall, muscular, and stunning, and he wore only two pieces of clothing: a pair of tight black pants and an exquisitely ornate mask covered in feathers and sequins.

She tried to sit up, but he knelt beside her, and once again, she felt his hands on her, steadying her.

"What . . . who . . . ?" was all she could manage.

185

He just smiled from under the mask with what looked like luscious lips. She couldn't see them very well, as the large mask, unfortunately, covered most of his face.

"Hold on to Marcel," he said. "I've got you."

Her body lurched again, but this time she realized it was because of the elaborately decorated Mardi Gras float upon which she was now riding down the streets of New Orleans. She was above the thronging masses, moving through the cool Louisiana night air, passing crowds of smiling faces.

She grinned and turned to gaze at the mysterious Marcel again, but he was gone. For a moment, she panicked, not out of fear, but out of longing. She had only seen him for a second, but knew she had to see more.

Unsure of what to do, she tried to stand, but the movement of the float knocked her back down on her bottom. Suddenly, out of nowhere, the hands were back, and they held tightly as they helped Melissa to her feet. She turned, and there he stood again.

"I needed more beads," he explained.

He handed Melissa a dozen strands or so, and she joined Marcel in tossing them to the crowd. Happy spectators cheered and waved at her, so she waved back at them, like she was Miss Mardi Gras. She never felt so wonderful.

Between throws, she watched her masked man covertly as he stretched his body out with each toss, his muscles rippling in the soft glow of the streetlights. He looked fine, mighty fine.

Suddenly the float jerked again, and Melissa fell into him. Whether it was accidental or intentional, she didn't care. All she knew was that she was being held in two very strong arms and looking at two very incredible eyes that riveted on her through the openings in the mask. They were the color of a blue-green tropical ocean; the kind you see in a picture on a travel brochure, and all she wanted to do was to dive into them.

"I can make you happy," he said.

"Right here? In front of everyone?" she stammered and felt herself turn a deep shade of red.

He laughed softly. "I mean, you don't have any beads." Then, with a devilish grin he added, "But you know what you need to do to get some, don't you?"

No! she thought to herself. He can't be another typical male!

He stepped closer and cupped his hand under her chin. "You just have to show me your . . . beautiful smile."

That she could do, and she gave him a dazzling one as he moved in to slowly, seductively drape several strands over her head and around her neck. He didn't move back once he was done, however. In fact, he moved in a little closer and held on even tighter as the float swayed them back and forth.

Melissa could have kissed him for being such a gentleman. That's not a bad idea, she thought, amazed at her own boldness. She arched up and brought her lips closer to his, but they couldn't make contact. That

186

blasted mask was in the way.

"Could I . . . take off your mask?" She was being so assertive, and she liked the feeling of power it gave her.

His incredible eyes bore into hers. "For a start, yes."

Melissa reached up slowly, grasping the mask in her hand. She hesitated a moment, never feeling so excited in her life. She desperately wanted to see his face, but she wanted this moment to last forever. It was like opening the best birthday present ever.

He pulled her even closer, and now his gorgeous, gorgeous eyes were all she could see. "Take it off," he said, barely above a whisper.

She felt like she couldn't breathe. "I need air!" she gasped, closing her eyes . . .

Suddenly, the booming voice of the police officer rattled in her ear. "People, back up! Give her some air!"

Melissa opened her eyes to see the drunken mass had returned around her, some staring, most just drinking. The police officer and his horse loomed over her, as they tried to keep the crowd from trampling her.

She sat up and struggled to get her bearings. Where was the float? Where were her beads? Where was Marcel?

"You all right, lady?" the policeman yelled to her. She nodded feebly. He reached down and hauled her unceremoniously to her feet. Once he saw she was upright and somewhat stable, that was good enough for him, and he maneuvered his horse through the mob in search of bigger problems.

A moment later, Nate returned. "Did I miss anything?" he asked, obliviously, handing her a bakery bag filled with Cajun spice muffins and a cup of beer.

"No!" she snapped, trying to shake off the embarrassment of passing out in public, although it was obvious no one cared but her. She knew she needed food before there was a repeat performance, so she pulled out a muffin and took a bite. It was spicy and hot—just as her masked man had been. She closed her eyes and tried to take herself back to the float, back to the beads, back to those eyes. She was almost there when, without warning, a large, inebriated man dressed as Pebbles Flintstone fell into her, flooding the entire contents of her beer cup down the front side of her shirt. When she jerked back, her muffins went flying off into the abyss of the crowd, never to be seen again.

Nate tried to help her wipe the beer off, but she smacked his hand away. "I'll go get you more!" he shouted as he took off, once again swallowed by the mob.

"On my next big birthday," Melissa screamed, unheard by anyone, "I'm buying a pony!"

midnight snack muffins makes 12–15 muffins

2 cups flour

½ cup sugar

½ brown sugar

½ teaspoon salt

2 teaspoons baking powder

1 cup crunchy peanut butter

2 eggs, slightly beaten

1 cup buttermilk

½ cup grape jelly

1. Preheat oven to 350 degrees.

2. In a large bowl, mix together dry ingredients (flour through baking powder). Using a pastry blender or fork, cut in peanut butter until mixture is crumbly. Form a well in the center. Set aside.

3. In a separate bowl, mix together eggs, buttermilk, and jelly until well blended. Pour into dry-ingredient well and stir until just moistened.

4. Lightly grease or paper-line muffin cups. Fill each cup ¾ full of batter. Bake 15 to 20 minutes, or until a toothpick comes out clean. Let cool 5 minutes before removing from pan.

188

if you like midnight snack muffins, then you'll love

Antonio

It's late, and a noise from the kitchen wakes you. You creep downstairs to find Antonio in search of a late-night snack. For you, however, his perfect body silhouetted in the glow of the refrigerator light is a feast for your eyes. Wearing only white silk pajama bottoms, he looks like a dream come true. He pulls out a muffin and a carton of milk. What does that say on the side of the carton? Got stud?

apple for the teacher muffins

makes 12 muffins

¼ cup salted butter, melted

¼ cup packed brown sugar

½ cup chopped pecans

2 cups flour

½ cup sugar

2 teaspoons baking powder

1 teaspoon baking soda

½ teaspoon salt

¼ teaspoon cinnamon

¼ teaspoon nutmeg

½ cup milk

¼ cup salted butter, melted

2 eggs, beaten

1 teaspoon vanilla extract

1 large Granny Smith apple, peeled and chopped

1. Preheat oven to 375 degrees.

2. In a small bowl, stir together ¼ cup melted butter, brown sugar, and chopped pecans. Spoon mixture evenly into lightly greased muffin cups. Set aside.

3. In a large bowl, mix together dry ingredients (flour through nutmeg). Form a well in the center. Set aside.

4. In a separate bowl, stir together milk, ¼ cup melted butter, eggs, and vanilla extract. Pour into dry-ingredient well and stir until just moistened. Fold in apples.

5. Fill each muffin cup 2/3 full with batter. Bake 15 to 20 minutes or until a toothpick comes out clean. Invert pan and serve muffins upside down.

if you like apple for the teacher muffins, then you'll love

Grady

Class is in session, and your teacher is Grady. He's six-foot-four, and every inch of him is a chapter in perfection. Luckily for you, the only subject he teaches is the History of Love, so get ready to pull an all-nighter. Maybe if you bring him an apple muffin, he will give you extra credit. Grady will make sure you never want to be dismissed from his study hall.

bring me love chocolate muffins

makes about 18 muffins

1. Preheat oven to 350 degrees.

2. In a large bowl, mix together dry ingredients (flour through baking soda).

3. Stir in chocolate chips. Form a well in the center. Set aside.

4. In a separate bowl, stir together butter, egg, milk, and vanilla extract. Pour into dry-ingredient well and stir until just moistened.

5. Lightly grease or paper-line muffin cups. Fill each cup ¾ full. Bake 15 to 20 minutes, or until a toothpick comes out clean. Cool 5 minutes before removing from pan.

1¾ cups flour

¾ cup sugar

½ cup cocoa powder

2 teaspoons baking powder

½ teaspoon baking soda

2 cups semisweet chocolate chips

½ cup salted butter, melted

1 egg, beaten

1¼ cups milk

2 teaspoons vanilla extract

193

Sinfully Sweet

It was almost eleven o'clock, and I still had a daunting list of errands: drop off the dry cleaning, mail a package at the post office, get the van a long-overdue oil change, and take a very unhappy Sir Fluffy to the cat groomer (which was sure to end painfully for me). All of this before picking up the kids from school, which meant homework, book reports, finish the "Gravity and You" science project, then off to soccer practice and ballet lessons. Somewhere in there was laundry to do, dinner to make, and a house to clean. I became exhausted just thinking about it.

My breakfast of a banana and the half piece of toast that my son didn't finish was wearing thin as I lugged a pile of clothes toward the dry cleaners. I needed a cart—or possibly a llama—like the sherpas use to take stuff up those big mountains. No, what I need is a personal assistant, I thought to myself, the kind bigwigs and celebrities have. She—wait, make that he—would be at my disposal for such mundane activities, such as this. Yes, I could see it in my mind: I would just snap my fingers and

say, "You, young man there, take my laundry to the dry cleaners, then get the car washed and waxed, then pick up my prescriptions at the pharmacy." Okay, so maybe I really could use some medication . . .

Of course, there were no parking spaces in front of the Zippy Cleaners, so I precariously transported the pile of clothes down to the strip mall. Passing the nail salon, a crazy idea flew in my head: I could stop in for a quick pedicure. It would only take an hour, I reasoned with myself, and I'd get to sit up high in one of those chairs and have someone pamper my toes. Maybe they'd even throw in a foot massage . . . Unfortunately, the idea was kicked back out by all the other tasks packed in my brain and vying for my time. I trudged on.

The next store was Bob's Liquor. Tempting, but counterproductive, I knew. Up next was the pet store. In their front window sat a large lizard of some sort. He stared at me from his glass cage, and I stared back. For a moment, I was envious. At least he doesn't have to worry about dry cleaning.

The next store greeted my nose before my body got there. It was Roy's Bakery, which made some of the best goodies in town. I slowed my pace from a crawl to a creep, allowing the thick, delicious aroma of fresh-baked goodies that emanated from inside

to swirl around me. I stopped and looked in the window to see the incredible treats being created within. I knew I didn't have the time, nor the will-power, to stop in, but just looking wouldn't hurt, right?

Suddenly, my desire for baked items changed to a different kind of desire. I no longer cared about the brownies or the cookies or the muffins, for there, inside the front bakery window, stood the most incred-ibly handsome young man. He wore all white, from his snug T-shirt to his form-fitting pants, topped off by his flour-dusted apron. Muscular arms bulged from his rolled-up sleeves, and I became somewhat mesmer-ized as I watched his huge biceps ripple slightly as he stirred a large bowl of a creamy chocolate batter.

He had the face of a Greek god—no, a Roman god. Or possibly a Nordic one. Pick a god, any god, because this guy could go up against the best of them in a handsome god competition. He was stunning. His skin was tanned, but not like he'd been sitting pool-side all day (although that was not an unpleasant im-age in my head). His hair, dark and slightly wavy, was neatly combed back, all except a stray lock which fell slightly over his eyes. I watched him as he pushed it back with his forearm, smudging his face with flour.

I bet he cleans up nicely, I thought.

He suddenly looked up, as if sensing my pierc-ing stare. Our eyes met, and it was as if I were caught in the powerful pull of two dark brown tractor beams. They were the color of the chocolate batter he stirred. Never before had I seen eyes that deep of a brown—I believe my jaw actually dropped. And just when I didn't think he couldn't look any more yummy, he smiled at me. Dazzling white teeth glinted behind his luscious lips as he tipped the bowl toward me. He mouthed something, but I'm not a good lip-reader. It looked like he said, "Want some?" I found myself smiling back and nodding a little too vigor-ously. If only he wasn't talking about the batter, I briefly thought, then quickly reminded myself I was married with three children, as evidenced by the pile of laundry I was slowly dropping on my feet.

He smiled again—did he just wink?—and left the room. The show was over, and I knew I should be moving on, but I needed a few seconds to compose myself. I leaned my forehead against the cool glass. Closing my eyes, I breathed in the sweet, intoxicat-ing aroma . . .

When I opened them again, my view of the bakery was gone. In its place was an airy sunroom made up of spotless windows that overlooked an exquisite flower garden. Solid beds of peonies, irises, geraniums, and roses of every hue created a dazzling riot of color in the morning sun. Hummingbirds and butterflies flitted through the warm air, dancing their carefully orches-trated ballet on the breeze.

I found myself stretched out on a smooth leather chaise, so soft it felt like I was sitting on a cloud. I was propped up by eiderdown pillows covered in hand-embroidered cases, probably stitched by me in my spare

196

time. Still in my white silk pajamas, I lazily looked at the clock and smiled—no need to get dressed yet.

At arm's reach was a cut crystal pitcher of brewed tea, chilled to perfection. I poured myself a glass, adding a sprig of fresh mint I had probably grown in my herb garden. As I sipped, I glanced through a fashion magazine while watching a heart-warming episode of *The Oprah Winfrey Show.*

"Maybe I should do something," I pondered aloud, but as I looked around my immaculately clean house, I realized there was nothing to do. Everything was in its place, in an orderly, clean, and shiny manner. I sighed contently. Ding, dang, dong . . .

The quiet calm of the morning was broken by the ring of the door chimes. My heart skipped a beat. He was back.

"Come in!" I called, albeit a little too anxiously. Sitting up a bit, I picked up the hand mirror on the table next to the chaise. I started running my fingers through my hair, but then realized it was already perfectly coiffed. My makeup was also impeccable. Not bad, I thought. Giving myself a smile of approval, I carefully set the mirror down.

The door opened. There stood Philippe. His large, dark physique just about filled the frame of the door. He was dressed all in white, which seemed to be his attire preference, as I couldn't recall seeing him in anything else, not that I didn't fantasize about the possibilities. In his arms were several packages of varying sizes, which caused his strong muscles to strain against his shirt. He entered and set the packages down.

"Are you finished already?" I asked, enjoying the view from my chaise. "Philippe, you are the best personal assistant—ever."

"Thank you, Ma'am," he said, flashing a beautiful smile.

"What would I ever do without you?" I asked, with all sincerity. "Let's hope you never have to find out," he said, still smiling but adding a cute little wink. He began opening the packages, almost in slow motion, so as to give me adequate time to appreciate the flex of each muscle.

"Did Sir Fluffy give you any problems?" I asked.

"No, Ma'am," he replied. "He was a real pussycat at the vet's, as usual. He just purred the whole time."

Strangely, I believed I was about to purr, too, as I watched him hang my dry cleaning in the closet. That side of him was pleasant to watch, as well. He returned to the pile of packages and retrieved a small, elegant bag.

"I made an extra stop," he said with a coy smile. "I hope you don't mind." Trust me, I didn't mind anything he did, as long as he did most of it in my presence. Philippe reached in and pulled out a beautiful, red heart-shaped box. He brought it to me and dropped to one knee. Slowly, he opened the box to reveal one perfect double chocolate muffin.

I took it from the box, reveling in how dark, rich, and heavy it felt in my hand. I took a bite, and the

bring me love chocolate muffins

197

chocolate, still warm, caressed my tongue and slid smoothly down my throat.

"Thank you, Philippe," I murmured. "You are the best."

"Oh, there are other ways of staying in shape besides going to a gym. Sometimes you've got to be creative with your workout," he said with a coy smile.

"The pleasure's all mine, Ma'am," he said. "Now, are you ready for your pedicure?"

"Yes!" I said, finding myself becoming all giddy. I watched him as he retrieved a small box full of nail polish and manicure implements from the bathroom. He brought them to the table beside my chaise and set them down.

"Let's get you into a better position," he said rather seductively. Taking my hand in his, he gently pulled me up, then leaned over me to reach the lever on the chair that adjusted the back. For a lingering moment, his body pressed against mine, and through those white clothes I could feel his white-hot, toned body.

"When do you have time to work out?" I blurted out.

"Oh, there are other ways of staying in shape besides going to a gym. Sometimes, you've got to be creative with your workout," he said with a coy smile. "Here, I'll show you."

Philippe leaned over me again and then scooped me up in his arms. He spun me around, making my head spin a bit. I was now mere inches from his face, and those brown eyes of his pierced my soul. I felt like I was flying, and I wished I could fly away with him.

He gently put me back in my chair and went about his work to get my pedicure ready. "How about this color today?" he asked, holding up a beautiful little bottle which held the perfect shade of pink.

"Ooh, I like it!" I exclaimed.

He slowly knelt down and took one of my feet into his big, strong hands. He began massaging it, starting at my toes, and then working all the way up to my knee. The sensation was almost too good to handle, and I feared I would melt—or ruin the pedicure before it was even started—right then and there.

"Feel good?" he asked, and I assumed he gathered from the series of moans that emanated from me that it did. "That's my job—to make you feel good, any way I can. Just let me know what you need, and I will be on it."

198

Oh, what a proposal that was. Yes, I could think of something he could get on. Maybe we could start slowly, as it appeared I had the whole day open. Right now, though, I needed him to address my most urgent need.

"Philippe, could we start with you first massaging my temples?" I asked, batting my eyelashes. "My head is just pounding, like someone's banging on it."

"Of course, whatever you desire," he whispered, as he gave my foot one last caress. He then rose gracefully and walked behind my chaise. Slowly, with hands trained by the angels, he reached for my head and began pressing his fingers against my skin, softly at first, then with just enough pressure to send a shiver straight down to my toes. It was helping, but . . .

BANG! BANG! BANG!

"Oh, ugh. It just won't go away, Philippe . . ."

BANG! BANG! BANG!

I opened my eyes. There, in front of me stood a not-so-pleasant woman on the other side of the bakery window. "Don't press your face against the glass!" she screeched at me, pointing at the window. "You're leaving smudges!"

I stepped back quickly and reality slapped me smack in the face. Gone were the sunroom and the eiderdown pillows. Gone was the foot massage. Gone was Philippe, my Philippe. Suddenly, the pile of dry cleaning seemed larger and heavier, and I struggled under the weight to keep it in my arms. Worst of all, I was completely mortified to see the cute bakery guy watching and smiling in amusement.

Gathering up my dignity, I dragged my pile of clothes inside the bakery, tripping over them as I reached the order counter. "A double chocolate muffin, please," I said, breathlessly. "Actually, better make it two."

about the authors

judi guizado lives in Rancho Cucamonga, California, with her husband and two children. She began her writing career in earnest after winning the coveted Golden Key Award for Best Writer in Mrs. Riddle's second grade class at El Camino Elementary School, sometime in the last millennium. She enjoys the beach, reading, and watching the first thirty minutes of movies before falling asleep.

gilda jimenez lives in Southern California with her family, most of whom are of a furry nature. She likes to spend her free time reading, painting, and cooking—but not at the same time.

shari hartz lives in Victorville, California, with her husband and two dogs. She has been in the field of education for seventeen years, both at the teaching and at the administrative level, where she has discovered the importance of writing. She enjoys teaching her second graders, going on vacation, and playing with her two pups.

tammy aldag lives in Lake Arrowhead, California, with her husband. She has been a professional photographer for twenty years, winning many awards for her work, the most recent being the 2007 Wedding Portrait Photographers International Accolade of Excellence. Her studio is located in Rancho Cucamonga, California. www.artisticimages4u.com.